Probably the saddest and best-known accident happened early on 10th September 1944 at Snab Lane, Ness. A Mosquito (HJ816) from No 60 OTU based at High Ercall, Shropshire crashed during air-to-ground gunnery practice on Burton Marsh bombing range. Both Pilot (F/O Guy Merson Templer) and Navigator (F/O Derek Allan Attwood) from the Royal New Zealand Air Force were killed on impact. Local residents were horrified at the appalling scene that greeted them on arrival at the site. The plane had caught fire and burnt out – the remains of the airmen were buried in the war graves plot of Blacon Cemetery in Chester.

In 1943, an Avro Anson crash-landed at Neston after the landing gear failed. The plane had to be taken away in pieces as it was straddling a hedge in Woodfall Lane.

A Fairey Swordfish, belonging to the Royal Navy, landed in a field near West Vale one evening in 1944. The pilot simply needed directions to the nearest airfield as he was lost! He was advised to follow the railway lines to Sealand. The local police telephoned the airfield to ask them to put the runway lights on as it was getting dark and to expect a visitor.

The final reported crash in the Neston area occurred at Parkgate after the war had ended on 16th November 1945. The circumstances of the crash remained a mystery to the residents who had visited the wreckage soon after impact to search for survivors but found no trace of any occupants. 50 years later the pilot, Walter Swain, re-visited the scene and explained the events leading up to the crash. Swain, piloting an Airspeed Oxford, had become lost in bad weather at night. His radio failed and his fuel was low so he decided to bale-out. He landed safely some distance away and became the only airman to survive a bale out from an Oxford up to that time.

Gordon Hodgson – December 2002.

Ref: Neston at War 1939-1945 – published by the Burton & Neston History Society, 1999.

Image: Mosquito Bomber/Fighter Bomber Units 1942-45, Bowman M. Osprey Combat Aircraft Series No. 4, 1998.

Previous publications

Burton in Wirral
Neston 1840–1940

Neston at War
1939–1945

edited by
Geoffrey W. Place

cover painted by
David Scott

The Burton and Neston History Society
1999

Published by
The Burton and Neston History Society

ISBN 0 9509145 2 5
© The Burton and Neston History Society, 1999

All rights reserved. No part of this publication may be reproduced, stored in a retrieval system, or transmitted, in any form or by any means, electronic, mechanical, photocopying, recording or otherwise, without the prior permission of the publishers.

Designed, copy-edited and set in Palatino by David Morris

Printed in Great Britain by
Bemrose Shafron Ltd, Chester

Table of Contents

		page
The origins of this book		*vii*
Chapter One	THE OUTBREAK OF WAR	1
Chapter Two	EVACUEES AND REFUGEES	11
Chapter Three	AIRCRAFT OVER NESTON	29
Chapter Four	AIR RAIDS	41
Chapter Five	ON DUTY: THE EMERGENCY AND VOLUNTARY SERVICES	57
Chapter Six	THE DEFENCES	73
Chapter Seven	FOOD	91
Chapter Eight	THE HOME FRONT: WORKING FOR THE WAR EFFORT	109
Chapter Nine	THE ARMED FORCES	127
Chapter Ten	PEACE AT LAST	151
Index		165

The names of the many local people who have generously shared their memories with us, and have provided information or advice, are included in the sources listed at the end of each chapter. And we are also very grateful to all those who have allowed us to make use of photographs or other documents to illustrate this book.

THE ORIGINS OF THIS BOOK

In 1995 a very successful exhibition was held in Neston Town Hall to commemorate the 50th anniversary of VE Day. Susan Chambers organized the exhibition and collected an impressive amount of information, from the records of Neston Urban District Council, from newspapers and from people who came to see the exhibition. The research group of the Burton and Neston History Society had just finished their book *Neston 1840–1940* and decided to provide a sequel about the war years, using but greatly extending the work started by Susan. We have sought to tell the story of the war years as experienced in the area of the former Neston Urban District Council, which included Neston, Parkgate, Little Neston, Ness, Burton and Willaston. We have also said something about Raby and Puddington, the sites of nearby anti-aircraft batteries.

You will see from the list of sources at the end of each chapter that we have spoken to a great many people, for whose help we are very grateful. Inevitably we have missed some of those we should have talked to, and we apologize to them. We also apologize to anybody whose memory may differ from our account, and we would just say that, when faced with two or three conflicting memories of the same event, we have done our best to sort out the probable facts.

The members of the research group were Susan Chambers, Susan Craggs, Clive Edwards, Edward Hilditch, Clare Johnson, Kate Kelly, David and Hilary Morris, Geoffrey and Valerie Place and David Scott. The actual writing was undertaken by Geoffrey Place and Edward Hilditch, as shown at the end of each chapter.

This book stands as a memorial to those who went to fight and did not return, to those who did return and had to piece together their lives again, and to the wives and families who had to endure long years of worry and hardship.

CHAPTER ONE

THE OUTBREAK OF WAR

On Sunday 3 September 1939, the Prime Minister, Neville Chamberlain, announced on the radio that Britain was at war with Germany. The news was no surprise to anyone. For at least a year it had seemed increasingly likely that our country could not avoid becoming involved in the ever more grim affairs of Europe. Since Adolf Hitler had come to power in Germany in 1933, the extreme nationalism and contempt for foreigners which characterized his Nazi party, together with a policy of violence and military rearmament, made a repeat performance of the Great War, *"the war to end wars"*, all too likely.

Italy under Mussolini invaded Abyssinia in 1935, and Hitler marched into the demilitarized Rhineland in 1936, while in Spain Franco's Fascists fought the Spanish Republic, assisted by both Italy and Germany. The Germans annexed Austria in the spring of 1938, and were clearly looking covetously at further land in central Europe, particularly Czechoslovakia, which had a large German minority. Chamberlain went to see Hitler three times in September 1938. From the third meeting in Munich he brought back the *"piece of paper"* which promised that Hitler intended no further expansion, and Chamberlain accepted this as *"peace with honour"*, at the expense of Czechoslovakia.

Few people believed that Hitler could be trusted, and Britain prepared for war. Neston with its nearby villages was regarded as a safe area, and although its people, like those everywhere else, prepared for the worst, nothing very dreadful happened here, and Neston was fortunate in seeing the war years in relative security. But, as Churchill was to say, *"The whole of the warring nations are engaged, not only soldiers, but the entire population, men, women and children. The fronts are everywhere."* This was quite true. Everyone, even the children, felt involved in the war effort, and this book describes the involvement of the people of Neston.

The plans for the defence of our country were dominated, as war loomed ever nearer, by three major threats. These were attack by poison gas, attack by airborne troops, and urban bombing of such severity that huge

Chapter One

As early as January 1939, Neston Urban District Council sent 'visitors' to compile a register of accommodation suitable for evacuees in the event of war.

losses of civilian life could be expected. The first two, mercifully, did not happen, and the third was nothing like as severe as the prophets foretold.

The fear of gas derived from the use by the Germans of poison gas during the First World War. As early as July 1936, Pamela Jackson, the local Red Cross organizer, was giving lectures on gas attacks. Gas masks were issued to the entire population, 38 million nationally, in the spring of 1939. On 25 April, *"All the children* [at the elementary school in Liverpool Road] *brought their gas masks to school this afternoon, and as they have not been fitted by the local ARP wardens, this was done at school."* Three days later the school arranged a gas mask drill. In the first months of the war, everybody carried a gas mask in a cardboard case. For those whose case fell to pieces, or who wanted something smarter, George Henry Lee's in Liverpool offered gas mask containers in various materials, from leatherette for 2s. 6d. to pigskin for a staggering 35s. By the spring of 1940, almost nobody was still carrying gas masks, but the threat of invasion in June 1940 brought them out again for a short while.

Roy Booth recalled, *"The war really hit us, when each member of the family was issued with gas masks. Mine was in a cardboard box with string to carry it over my shoulder. I was told to take it everywhere I went."* Colin Foote described his gas mask as a big improvement on the primitive model kept by his Uncle Bill from the First World War. Colin's was

> *a rubber mask with Perspex eyepieces completely covering the face. One breathed through a circular filter about three inches long which hung down below the chin. There were frequent rehearsals in classroom and shelter to get used to the thing: no problem for most, but initially terrifying for some children. Exhaled breath under slight pressure escaped over one's cheeks, sometimes with a noise akin to breaking wind. This caused hilarity, which in turn caused the sight window to mist, so one was in a perpetual fog. The masks also induced sweating, and it was always a relief to take them off.*

Special gas masks, or respirators as they were called officially, were provided for babies, and for toddlers up to three years old, who had Mickey Mouse faces on theirs (280 in Neston). These were not given out until March 1940, although the council had been storing them for several months. In July 1940 improved filter caps were fitted to the gas masks, and for Neston children this was done at school.

> **17545**
>
> **COUNTY of CHESTER.**
> **AIR RAID PRECAUTIONS.**
>
> This is to certify that Geoffrey S. Boston, Esq.,
> of Hadlow Wood, Willaston,
> Wirral, Cheshire.
> has this day been duly appointed as an AIR RAID WARDEN and is hereby authorised to carry out the duties laid upon Wardens by the Chief Constable of Cheshire.
>
> ....Major.
> Chief Constable of Cheshire.
>
> Date of issue of card ... 1 AUG 1939
> Signature of Warden Geoffrey S. Boston.

Air raid wardens were also appointed before the outbreak of war.

Mustard gas (dichlorodiethyl sulphide), which causes blisters and affects the eyes, throat and lungs, was described in the official ARP manual as *"highly destructive to all living tissues"*. It would be dropped or sprayed as a liquid which would then evaporate. As it has little smell, a yellow-green paint was devised which would turn red if mustard gas liquid fell on it. David Scott remembers that this paint was put on the top of Royal Mail pillar boxes. It was also painted on boards at such places as military

Chapter One

barracks. The ARP manual listed two types of tear gas, three nose-irritant gases, three lung-irritant gases, two blister gases (including mustard gas) and one affecting the blood. Vincent Crook, who ran the chemist's and post office in Parkgate, was provided with ointment, bleach cream, to protect the skin from blister gas. This he put in a bucket with a lid outside his shop, as all chemists' shops did, for people to help themselves. After a few weeks the authorities took the bucket away. The *Birkenhead News* advised its readers to lay in a stock of bleach powder for the skin, and antiseptic lotion for the eyes, as an antidote to gas. Fortunately the Germans did not use any gas in their attacks: possibly they knew that this country had its own stockpile of poison gas. RAF pilots were trained to spray invading troops on the beaches with gas, although its use had been outlawed by the Geneva Gas Protocol of 1925.

The second major fear at the outbreak of war was attack by airborne troops. It was known that the German army was perfecting the *Blitzkrieg*, or lightning war, although we did not appreciate how lightning it was until the Germans sped across France and Belgium in May 1940 and pinned our army at Dunkirk. The first duty of the Home Guard was to tackle airborne invaders. To this end road blocks were prepared, pillbox forts were built and obstacles were placed on open spaces where planes or gliders might try to land. One strange symptom of this fear of paratroops was seen in the removal of any sign which might tell a stranger where he was. Bill Jones recalled,

> *I can remember all town and village name signs being taken down, and all shops and vans with local names or addresses had to have them obliterated: for example, Neston Laundry, and Little Neston Post Office. Any stranger asking the name of a town he was in would have soon caused suspicion, as everybody was drilled mentally to observe everything and to remember that 'careless talk costs lives'.*

The police were vigilant in looking for suspicious characters, as Norman Thelwell, the artist, found out. He lived in Prenton, and at the age of 16 or 17 would cycle all over Wirral, including the Neston area, sketching whatever he saw:

> *It was great fun being cornered by police cars once the war had started. They would question my motives for making drawings of churches, farms or even a few cows in a field, with hands up while they went through my pockets and the inevitable, 'Don't you know there's a war on? All right then, son, but watch your step.'*

They did not confiscate his drawings, but from one of his friends they

AIR RAID PRECAUTIONS

* The A.R.P. Warden's Post for your Sector is:

_____

_____

* The nearest First Aid Post is:

_____

_____

* THESE TWO POSTS WILL ALWAYS BE MANNED DURING AIR RAIDS.

Help or advice upon A.R.P. matters will be given by the local wardens.

The nearest SENIOR WARDEN is:

_____

_____

Ask him for the name and address of your nearest local Warden and make a note of it here:

_____

_____

Get to know him *now* and note any changes in the names and addresses given here.

IN CASE OF INJURY
Wounded and gas contaminated casualties who can walk should go direct to the nearest First Aid Post. If you suspect that your clothing has been contaminated by liquid gas, remove the affected garment immediately and place it outside the house, then wash yourself thoroughly. Stretcher cases will be taken to hospitals.

GAS MASKS
TAKE CARE OF YOUR GAS MASK. Learn how to put it on and take it off and how to store it properly. Keep it ready for immediate use. If you have no gas mask or if your mask does not fit or seems out of repair, speak to your Warden about it at once.

LIGHTING RESTRICTIONS
All windows, doors, skylights or openings which would show a light, must be screened so that no light can be seen from outside. Do not use a light in a room unless the blind or curtain is drawn, and remember that a light at the back of the house is just as visible from the air as one at the front.

AIR RAID WARNING SIGNALS
● WARNING SIGNAL. *Warbling or intermittent sound on siren; Whistles blown by police and wardens.* ● GAS WARNING. *Rattles sounded.* ● RAIDERS PASSED. *Continuous sound on siren.* ● ALL CLEAR. *Handbells rung.*
When you hear the WARNING Signal TAKE COVER AT ONCE and stay there until you hear the continuous sound on the siren or the ringing of a handbell. Have your Gas Mask with you. If RATTLES have been used warning you of gas, do not come out until you hear HANDBELLS.

FIRE PRECAUTIONS
Be ready to deal with an incendiary bomb. Clear all lumber from your attic NOW, and see that you have easy access to the attic or roof space. Provide two buckets filled with water and, if possible, a stirrup hand pump with two-purpose nozzle, either producing spray for dealing with the bomb itself, or producing a jet for tackling the resulting fire.
Have a reserve supply of water in buckets or tubs. Leave used water in bath.
If you have no stirrup hand pump, have two buckets of sand or dry earth near the top of the house, and a shovel with a long handle for putting sand on the bomb. After covering the bomb with sand place it in a bucket which has a few inches of sand in the bottom, and remove it from the house. Scrape up every particle of burning metal. The resulting fire will then have to be extinguished. Buckets of water or a folded blanket kept wet from a bucket of water might be used.
On no account throw water on the bomb or an explosion may result.
If you cannot put out the fire send for help to

_____

_____

★ **HANG THIS CARD IN A PERMANENT AND PROMINENT POSITION**

Notices like this were distributed to inform and remind people what action to take to avoid or deal with hazards. Although gas and incendiary devices are mentioned, it is surprising that there is no specific reference to high-explosive bombs.

took a much-folded magazine picture of the swimming star, Esther Williams, for further examination.

Local people feared that the flat expanse of the Dee marshes might offer an attractive landing ground for enemy paratroops (though the military authorities did not, apparently, share this fear). Neston Council thought that the black and white frontage of Mostyn House School in Parkgate was too conspicuous a landmark, and deputed a councillor to suggest to the headmaster, A. M. D. Grenfell, that he should camouflage it with grey paint. But he had flown his own plane before the war, and could show that from a flying height the black and white stripes did not show up.

As with the fears of gas attack, the Germans did not use paratroops against Britain and had no plans to do so. The tactics of *Blitzkrieg* required airborne troops to be speedily reinforced by tanks, which was not possible unless a seaborne invasion had already taken place.

Neston began to prepare for the possibility of war following a letter from the Home Office in June 1935 about air raid precautions, generally referred to as ARP. This reflected the third fear, that the massive bombing of cities would cause enormous civilian casualties. For this reason the evacuation of children from the danger areas to safe places like Neston was planned weeks before war broke out. In May 1939 the council school in Burton Road was closed for two days to prepare for the influx of evacuees, including the storage of emergency food. The first and largest wave of evacuation took place the day before war was declared. There had been a Cheshire County Council conference on air raid precautions in March 1936 at Crewe, after which three Neston councillors were appointed to report on ARP. In February 1937 a public meeting on the subject was held in Neston, and in the same year Parliament passed an Air Raid Precautions Act which obliged local authorities to take this responsibility. In March 1938 the council formed an ARP committee, but it could do little at that stage, because Neston, being an 'unspecified area' (that is, not in danger), did not have priority for funds, particularly as regards shelters, from the county. This committee was reconstituted in January 1939 as a Civil Defence committee, and in the following August an Emergency Committee was created, with full powers to act in all matters of emergency in connection with Civil Defence. The provision of shelters was a slow business, but schools were provided with shelters first. Mostyn House School built its own shelter in the spring of 1939.

Even the threatened mass bombing was not, in the event, as bad as was predicted. Terrible though the destruction was in Liverpool, Bootle,

The interior of Mostyn House school's air raid shelter was palatial in its dimensions. It was fitted with bunks in anticipation of night-time raids. When this photograph was taken after the war, it was being used as a store room.

Wallasey and Birkenhead, as well as other cities like Coventry and Plymouth, and above all in London, the damage done by German bombers to Britain was by no means as devastating as the appalling destruction which Allied bombers wreaked on Germany. As Air Marshal 'Bomber' Harris said, *"The Germans sowed the wind."* They certainly reaped the whirlwind. After Liverpool's worst eight days, the 'May blitz' in 1941, rumours spread that 50,000 had been killed: the actual figure was about 1,900.

In 1914, at the outbreak of the First World War, many people in Britain thought that war, fought between armed forces of professional soldiers and sailors, would have a cleansing, beneficial effect, and many of the early volunteers went to fight in a spirit of patriotic adventure. There was no such eagerness for battle in 1939, but rather a spirit of grim determination. In June 1939, as a timely reminder to Merseyside of the realities of armed combat, the submarine HMS *Thetis* sank off the coast of North Wales. The *Thetis* was built in Birkenhead by Cammell Laird, and

Chapter One

on 1 June 1939 it left the Mersey for diving trials in Liverpool Bay. On board were the crew of five officers and 48 ratings, with a further 53 observers, including 26 employees of Cammell Laird — 103 men in all. The submarine would not dive because it had too much buoyancy. The auxiliary tanks were flooded with water but the boat still would not dive. The torpedo officer thought that two of the six torpedo tubes, which should have been flooded, were empty because no water trickled out when he opened a testing hole. But the test hole had been clogged with paint and when he opened the torpedo tube, sea water rushed into the submarine because the tube's bow cap had been left open. The front compartment of the submarine filled with water and it sank. Four men reached the surface through the escape hatch, but the escape mechanism then jammed. With twice the normal complement aboard, the carbon dioxide level rose to the point where it killed the remaining 99 men. It took four months to raise the boat and remove the dead. One of the victims had a sister at Leighton School in Parkgate, and Lilian Williams remembered the shock and distress of the girls when they heard the news. Members of Neston Council stood in silent memory of two of the victims who were local men. They were the senior naval officers on board: Lieutenant-Commander G. H. Bolus, in command of *Thetis*, lived at Willaston, while Lieutenant-Commander R. N. Garnett, in command of the sister ship *Taku*, lived at Ness.

In March 1939 Hitler invaded Czechoslovakia. His next target was clearly Poland, and Britain and France promised to support that country. Britain was rapidly rearming, and announced that conscription would be introduced. On 24 August Parliament passed the Emergency Powers (Defence) Act, which gave the Government power to do almost anything, and within the next few days a hundred or so regulations were issued. On 1 September Germany invaded Poland. The evacuation of children, expectant mothers and those with babies, and disabled people began from the large cities. People tend to remember where they were when the Prime Minister, Chamberlain, announced that the country was at war on 3 September. Harry Sowden had just come out of St Winefride's church, with his wife and six children, when a man told him the news. *"Of course, the news was not unexpected. All kinds of preparations had been going on for quite some time."*

As soon as Roy Booth heard the news,

I went out on my bike and had to tell someone. When I got to Little Neston railway station I saw a schoolfriend called Bernard Coles. When I told him, he said, 'Perhaps the Germans will bomb our school and we won't have to go any more.' I thought that a great idea at the time, but I was only eleven, and children of six have more sense today than we did at eleven.

Colin Foote had a more sombre memory:

My mother had been a schoolgirl during the First World War and her anguished sobs following Chamberlain's radio announcement were heartrending. I remember them well, and also my brother and me trying to console her. She feared that Dad, who was out at the time, would be 'taken away from us', which in view of a recent 'licking' I thought might be no bad thing at that point.

Chapter One

SOURCES

This section was written by Geoffrey Place. The national background has been gleaned from Angus Calder, *The People's War*. The preparations for war in Neston were researched by Susan Chambers from council documents and newspapers. The details of HMS *Thetis* come from C. E. T. Warren and J. Benson, *The Admiralty Regrets*.

We are grateful for the memories of Roy Booth, Vincent Crook, Colin Foote, Bill Jones, Harry Sowden, Norman Thelwell and Lilian Williams.

Air Raid Precautions Handbook No.1, Personal protection against gas, was kindly provided by Tom Jackson.

CHAPTER TWO

EVACUEES AND REFUGEES

Neston received several waves of evacuees. The first wave, children from Wallasey, came in September and October 1939. The next wave, children from Guernsey, came in June 1940. As bombing destroyed houses on Merseyside, other evacuees came to Neston in 1940 and 1941. And finally, children from London came to Neston in 1944, mainly in July and later months. In addition, several firms from Liverpool set up offices in Neston.

By the first three days of September 1939, three and a half million children had been evacuated from those large cities deemed to be in danger to safe areas in the country. Neston's share of this vast migration was two trainloads of children from Wallasey, while other Wallasey children were sent to Heswall and Hawarden. Most of these children lived in the dockland areas of Poulton and Seacombe. They were sent by schools, and the Neston contingent came from two schools, Poulton and Riverside. Of course, quite a number of parents would not allow their children to leave home, and none of the Wallasey schools actually closed.

Frank Poole, the Neston Town Clerk, was in charge of billeting (as he was of many other aspects of Civil Defence), and his deputy was Albert Tilley. Lists of billets were drawn up and it was then the task of a team of women volunteers to place the children, although some thought they lacked the necessary authority and asked that they might act as assistants to male billeting officers. Under the emergency regulations, householders could be compelled to accept evacuees, but it was hardly sensible to force people to take children against their will, and some refused. Some others were reported to be disappointed that they did not get a child (for whom they would have been paid a living allowance). When the children arrived on 2 September, they were all placed within two hours. A group of them were brought to Parkgate and assembled in the covered playground at Mostyn House School. Betty Pritchard and a helper took the tearful children to the addresses they had been given, trying to keep brothers and sisters together, although this was not always possible. They found it a heartbreaking task. One householder in Manorial Road, Miss

Hayes, took in two mothers with two babies, but there was only one cot. So Mrs Pritchard drove one of the mothers back to Wallasey to her house near the gasworks, to fetch a cot. The mothers did not like Parkgate because there was no fish and chip shop, and they soon returned home.

The evacuees arrived on a Saturday. The next day Mary Chrimes, who worked for Neston Council, was summoned:

> *I had a phone message to go into work on Sunday 3 September* [the day the war started]. *I worked in an old pub called The Vaults, opposite the town hall, answering visiting parents' questions on where the children had been billeted. Mr Foote, the rating officer, was in the bar, also speaking to parents.*

The Wallasey children had their own teachers with them, Mr H. S. Booker and Mr Orde. At first they went to the local elementary schools which ran a shift system. Doreen Chrimes remembers

> *going to school in the mornings only one week and in the afternoons only the following week for a blissful period at the beginning of the war. The evacuees used the school when the Neston children were not there. I don't know how long this arrangement lasted — too brief a time for a child, I imagine.*

Wallasey Education Committee rented several local halls for the schooling of their children. The main one in Neston was the Congregational Hall (the former chapel on the site now occupied by the British Legion), requisitioned in December, which suggests that Mrs Chrimes's bliss lasted for most of the autumn term. They also rented St Winefride's hall next to the Roman Catholic church, and the Gladstone Village Hall at Burton. As the numbers dropped, the children at Burton were absorbed into the local school the following February. In Willaston they used the local school until February 1940, when the church hall was hired for them.

Back in Wallasey, Elleray Park special school remained closed for the first five weeks of term. When it reopened on 9 October, 39 of the children were brought to Rigby House in Parkgate by their headmistress, Miss R. Taylor, and her assistant, Miss Millington, while 31 children remained at Elleray Park. Rigby House was the building formerly used as a convalescent home by Chester Royal Infirmary. When they sold it in 1925 it became partly flats and partly a holiday home for children. Miss Taylor brought helpers with her, including Nurse Ogle. Dr Yeoman used to tell a tale that the nurse at Rigby House appealed to him for medicines. At least she would not need laxatives, he replied, *"because these are evacuated children"*. Perhaps it was Nurse Ogle who was the butt of his wit.

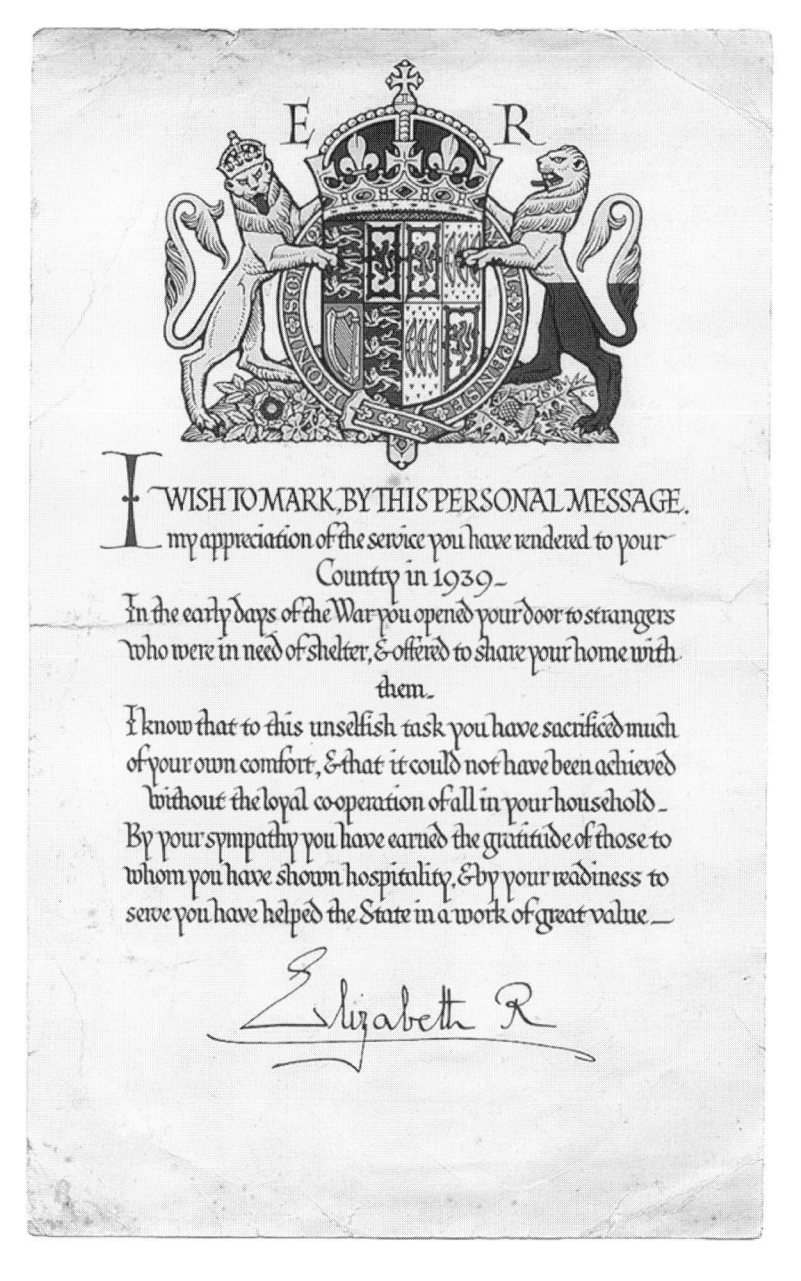

> I WISH TO MARK, BY THIS PERSONAL MESSAGE, my appreciation of the service you have rendered to your Country in 1939.
>
> In the early days of the War you opened your door to strangers who were in need of shelter, & offered to share your home with them.
>
> I know that to this unselfish task you have sacrificed much of your own comfort, & that it could not have been achieved without the loyal co-operation of all in your household.
>
> By your sympathy you have earned the gratitude of those to whom you have shown hospitality, & by your readiness to serve you have helped the State in a work of great value.
>
> *Elizabeth R*

Official recognition of people's contribution to the war effort in so many ways was marked by the issue of certificates which formally expressed the thanks of the King or Queen.

Chapter Two

For the first six months after war was declared, nothing happened so far as Britain was concerned: this was the period of the 'phoney war', or 'bore war'. Parents soon began to reclaim their children, some after only a few days. This was not just because there seemed to be no danger, but also because there were differences of cultural expectation between what we now call the 'inner city' and a small rural town.

One problem was diet, and the condemnation of Parkgate for its lack of fish and chips has already been noted. Two children arrived at Mrs Lettice Crossley's house in Willaston with a tin of corned beef and a block of chocolate. When the evening meal appeared they demanded their own rations first. Jessie Pritchard, who ran a newsagent's shop, had two boys billeted with her. She thought them inadequately dressed for school, so she went to Birkenhead and bought each of them a blazer out of her own pocket, but the boys refused to wear them. Some evacuees, such as Miss Piper, a teacher from London, hated the quiet of the countryside. She stayed a month only. Because the Wallasey children were near their homes, some were very homesick and did not settle. Nor was this only true of the children. Mrs Marie Crook had a mother with a baby billeted with her in Parkgate, but the husband could not cope on his own in Wallasey. His wife thought he was drinking and not looking after himself, so she returned home.

A few householders complained that their charges were *"dirty"*. This may have reflected the fact, discovered by many thousands of foster-parents throughout the country, that children suddenly uprooted from their homes are apt to wet the bed. As Kathleen Byrne, an infant teacher who took her Birkenhead children to Wrexham, explained, *"Strange surroundings, different food, they had nightmares (the Germans were coming), there was blackout on the windows and they could not see any street lights — no wonder they wet the bed."* Occasionally the problem may have been worse than this. It was found nationally that perhaps 10% of children from slum areas were inadequately toilet-trained and were liable to relieve themselves in inappropriate places. Two Neston householders have implied that they encountered this problem, and one of them asked their father to remove his two children billeted with her.

Such difficulties were rare. The evacuees who stayed seem to have fitted in well. *"We all integrated and played together,"* Colin Foote reflected, *"there was no friction whatsoever."* At Christmas 1939 there was a fancy dress party at the Institute (now the Civic Hall) for the Wallasey evacuees staying in Neston. There were 250 there including the hosts. The winner of the over-10s contest was dressed as Hitler.

The children at Rigby House returned to Elleray Park in April 1940 as there seemed to be no danger. It was after their return that their school had to be closed for several weeks because of a time-bomb in the grounds. Other evacuees were to come to Neston from Merseyside later in the war. Dot Burrows was sent here after the Christmas raids in December 1940, aged ten. Her father, a ferry captain living in New Brighton, had been injured on Christmas Eve while trying to extinguish an incendiary bomb with sand outside his house. Dot was sent to stay with her uncle, Herbert Hughes, the manager of the brickworks in Leighton Road, while her brother went with his school to Nantwich. All the Neston schools were full, so she joined Mr Vining's evacuee school at the Institute. Like many evacuees, she found rural Neston a completely new experience. *"I loved wandering round the brickworks and watching the bricks being made, taking my three-year-old cousin through the fields collecting primroses and bluebells."* Dot found that her dance teacher, Miss Mooney, had also found refuge in Neston after her dancing school in Wallasey was bombed. Dot found the Neston people very friendly. William Jackson, an elderly gentleman who lived at Leighton Court, used to invite her into his garden and give her apples.

Some people escaped temporarily from the perils of bombing, either by leaving the cities at night or by seeking a few days' respite in the countryside. Stanley Edge, a butcher in New Ferry, used to come out to Raby every night to stay at Corner House Farm to avoid the raids.

When the raids on Liverpool intensified in March 1941, the Neston Hotel, which stood opposite the town hall, was requisitioned (apart from the billiard room) for the use of evacuees. On 1 February 1941 Miss Taylor had brought 31 children back to Rigby House for a second evacuation from Elleray Park, and they stayed in Parkgate for eighteen months.

Muriel Grantham came to live, first in Willaston, and later in Moorside Lane, Neston, after their house in Wallasey was bombed. The same disaster happened to William Walker and his wife Phyllis. Captain Walker had won an MC in the First World War, and he became adjutant of the Wirral Home Guard sector. When the Home Guard acquired The Mount at Hinderton as their sector headquarters, the Walkers lived in a flat there. Some evacuees remained in Neston permanently. Irene Cottrell was to marry a Neston man, while Joe Birkett, whose stepmother was bombed out of two successive houses in Wallasey, remained in Neston where he had made his friends and worked for the Post Office.

The Germans invaded the Channel Islands on 30 June 1940. Just beforehand, on 21–24 June, 28,000 people were evacuated from the Islands. Of these about fifty from Guernsey came to the Neston area, and unlike other evacuees, they could not go home until 1945. Marie Batiste was only six:

> *What an upheaval for families when the evacuation started! Parents were encouraged to send their children to England, on the understanding that they would join them later. One of my sisters had already left for Bury, as she worked at the children's home and was looking after the babies, and two other sisters were going with the school. There were so many people and few boats, so after Mum had said goodbye, the girls came back home and were told to be ready at 6 a.m. the next day. On hearing the talk about a holiday and going on a big boat, I also wanted to go. I was six years old, and after a lot of thought it was decided that I would go and my mother would follow later. I was very excited, not understanding the implications. My elder sister, aged 13, was very upset at leaving Mum.*

Charlie Le Prevost, who was nearly ten at the time, remembered seeing German reconnaissance planes over Guernsey before they left. He had to take a pillowcase containing a change of clothes, soap, flannel and toothbrush. Like most of the Guernsey children who came to Neston, he had attended St Saviour's School, whose headmaster, Mr G. Vining, and other teachers came with them. They travelled on a cargo ship, the *Viking*, from St Peter Port to Weymouth. On the voyage, to the great excitement of the boys who thought there was an enemy submarine about, the ship was put on full alert. The children then boarded a train, having never seen one before, for an unknown destination which turned out to be Lancashire. Several hundred children arrived in Eccles, and lived for a fortnight in Brotherton Hall, where they slept two to a camp bed. Most of the children seem to have disliked this period. It was not just that the people spoke in a Lancashire dialect that seemed like a foreign language: some of the children spoke Guernsey patois and had only learned English at school. Nor did they like the food. For Barbara Tostevin, *"The fortnight in Eccles seemed like a bad dream."* The meal they were given on arrival at Neston Town Hall (Nancy Moore remembers chips and peas) was *"our first proper meal since leaving home two weeks before."*

Most of the Guernsey children were to be billeted in industrial areas around Manchester, and the fifty or so children who were sent to rural

Neston were the lucky ones. They arrived by train on Sunday 7 July. After their meal the children had to stand in line while prospective foster-parents chose the ones they liked the look of. If they were not chosen, one of the WVS ladies took them away:

> *The hall is thinning out — a lady asks me if I have been chosen. No, I haven't. A schoolfriend next to me has not been chosen either. The lady says, 'You had better come along with me then', and takes us a short distance in her car, stops and says, 'Right, one here, one next door.' I say to Joy, 'You go there, I'll go here.' What a way to decide where you are probably going to live for the next five years plus. What a blessing we did not know just how long our exile would last.*

Anne Millington remembered this process from the residents' point of view:

> *My mother volunteered to take children from Guernsey. The day of arrival is still very clear. The authorities arrived with two children for Mum to choose whom she would take, out of Jimmy, a boy of 7, and a girl of 9. Before my mother could answer, the little boy said, with tears in his eyes, 'My mum said we have not got to be parted.' They were brother and sister. We had them for five years and seven months. My mother received five shillings a week to clothe and feed each child. Hard times: first up, best dressed, but plenty of fun.*

The next day all the Guernsey children were taken to the council school in Burton Road. Those children who were Roman Catholics, together with two nuns from Les Cotils convent school, went to St Winefride's, where the church hall had been requisitioned for them. The rest were to go with the headmaster of St Saviour's, Gerald Vining, and his assistant, Ada Torode. However, there were too many to be integrated into the council school, and the children were told to go back to their new homes—but Nancy and Joy had to find their own way from Burton Road to Leighton Road:

> *'Return to your billets.' Yes, well, a pity Joy and I had not yet discovered the names of the people we were billeted with and no one had thought to tell us their address. Oh dear! Some while later, with me dragging a tearful Joy (anything but joyful) by the hand, I was greatly relieved to find the houses we had arrived at the previous afternoon.*

It was soon established that the Guernsey children would be taught in two rooms in the Institute, which had previously been used as overflow accommodation for infants from the council school. Mr Vining visited the local schools to scrounge all the spare furniture and materials he could

> **From:** WAR ORGANISATION OF THE BRITISH RED CROSS AND ORDER OF ST. JOHN
>
> **To:** Comité International de la Croix Rouge Genève
>
> Foreign Relations Department.
>
> Expéditeur SENDER Absender
>
> Name: PRIAULX
> Christian name: BURNICE MAUD
> Address:
>
> MESSAGE Mitteilung
> (Not more than 25 words)
>
> DEAR DAD
> HOPE YOU WELL (SEE WILLMA - GIVE LOVE) RECEIVED MESSAGES - GLAD YOU SAFE. GOT NEW CLOTHES - FOOD GOOD PLENTY. LOVE ALL
> BERNICE
>
> Date: MARCH 24th 1943
>
> Destinataire ADDRESSEE Empfänger
>
> Name: PRIAULX
> Christian name: CLIFFORD
> Address: BAS COURTIL
> ST SAVIOURS
> GUERNSEY C.I.

Above and facing page: The importance of personal communication between the Guernsey evacuees and their parents must have far outweighed the paltry number of words allowed and the flimsiness of the forms provided.

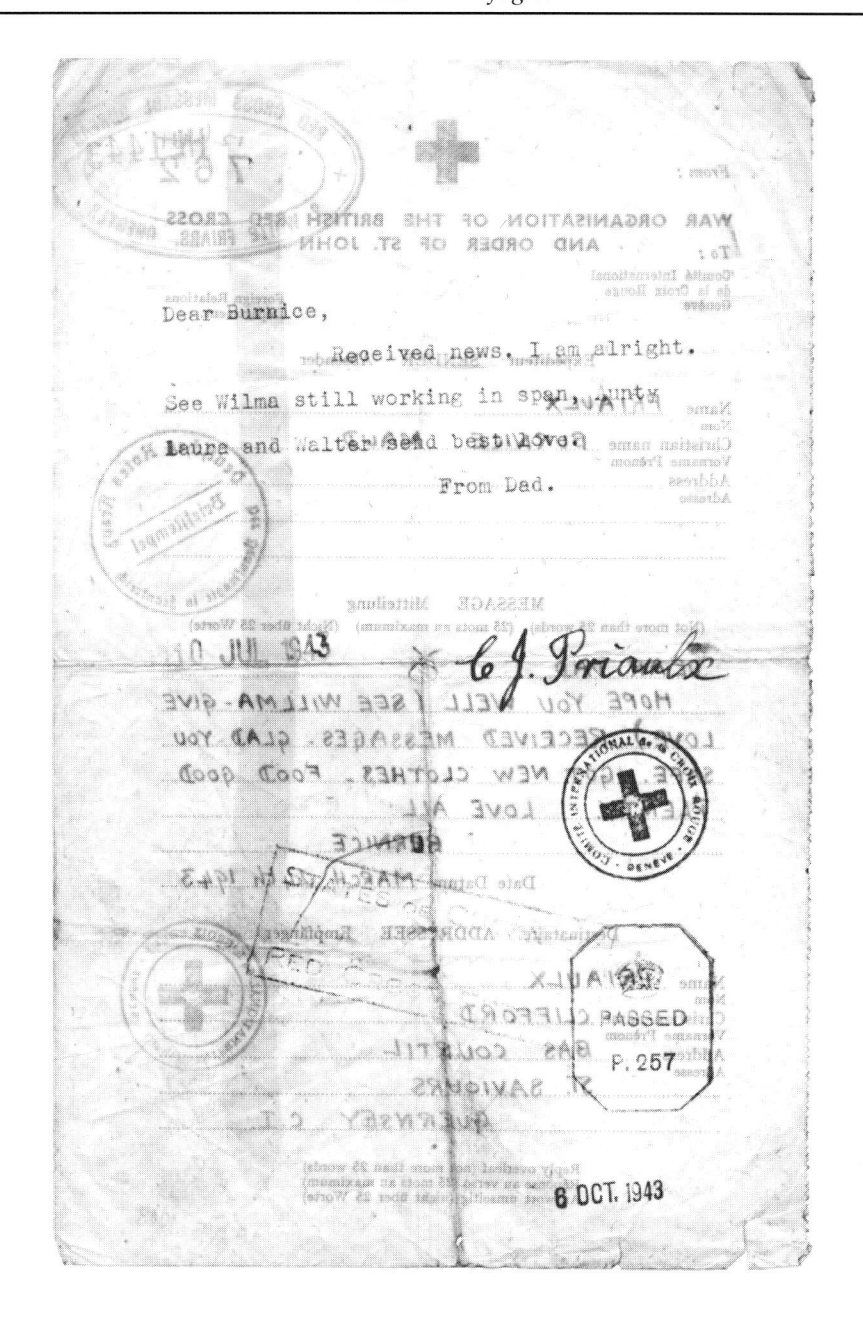

WAR ORGANISATION OF THE BRITISH RED CROSS
AND ORDER OF ST. JOHN

Dear Burnice,

　　　　Received news. I am alright.

See Wilma still working in span, Aunty

Laura and Walter send best love.

　　　　　　From Dad.

HOPE YOU WELL. I SEE WILMA. GIVE
LOVE. RECEIVED MESSAGES. GLAD YOU
HAVE NEW CLOTHES. FOOD GOOD.
　　　　　　LOVE ALL
　　　　　　BURNICE

Date Datum MARCH 2ND 1943

Destinataire ADDRESSEE Empfänger

Name VAULX
Christian name CLIFFORD
Address BAS COURTIL
　　　ST SAVIOURS
　　　GUERNSEY C.I.

6 OCT. 1943

lay his hands on. He is remembered with affection as a kind but strict and effective teacher: a large, sandy-haired man who taught the upper class while Miss Torode took the lower. He also took children from Burton Road for swimming lessons at the Parkgate baths. His wife was with him, and Mrs Vining is remembered helping to sort clothes provided by the Red Cross. There were some playground battles between the Guernsey children and the Wallasey children from the Congregational chapel school next door, but Mr Booker's school soon closed and its remaining pupils transferred to Mr Vining's care at the Institute in September. One of these pupils, for six months in 1941, was Dot Burrows, in whom he instilled a love of literature. In December 1940 there was a Grand Christmas Party in the town hall provided by the WVS, with 50 Guernsey children one day and 50 Wallasey children the next. There was a substantial tea and a conjuror, as well as presents from a tree provided by Miss Bulley.

Not everything was rosy at the evacuee school. One boy remembered playing truant, keeping watch on the playground from a wooded mound to judge when it was dinner time or home time. Many of the children suffered from an outbreak of boils, perhaps a result of their poor diet in Eccles, and the same boy had to attend the hospital in Little Neston each day for the treatment of eight boils on his backside.

Not all the Guernsey children arrived at the same time. Marion Tostevin was six when she left home, speaking little English. She was sent to Bolton, where she was separated from her sisters and was very unhappy. Her foster-parents punished her excessively, and she was moved to Neston in July 1942. Here she met with a great deal of kindness, but at first she knew nobody, not even the Guernsey children.

Eventually the children were able to write and receive very brief letters, 25 words only, to their parents in Guernsey via the Red Cross. *"There were many rumours of what the Germans were doing in the Channel Islands, and my foster-parents got very upset, but I really did not understand."* But some of the children were more fortunate as their parents had also got away. One little girl was only five when she was brought to Neston. Her parents were in St Helens and eventually traced their daughter. When her father came to fetch her, she had forgotten him, so he had to find Mr Vining and returned with a policeman and permission to take her back to St Helens, where they spent the rest of the war.

Many of the evacuees were impressed by the novelty of their new surroundings:

Some of the things and places I saw for the first time stand out in my memory: rivers, mountains, snow; Chester and its cathedral; Liverpool, and crossing the Mersey by ferry and underground. A whole new world opened up for me. Events which I recall were days spent in the air raid shelter at school and nights under the stairs at home; a Christmas party in the town hall; an outing to Southport and being disappointed not to see the sea, also a donkey ride which I did not enjoy! Sunday School when I was taught by Miss Lee and Miss Marle; confirmation classes at the vicarage (Rev. Frank Bennett) and confirmation in Neston parish church.

Bob Tostevin enjoyed cycling around the countryside, and learned to milk a cow at Raby. But he suffered dreadfully from the unaccustomed cold, especially in the severe winter of 1941–2. He hated the Saturday morning children's film show, the 'tuppenny rush', in Neston's New Cinema, to which he was sent for his supposed amusement, with "*hundreds of screaming children jumping up and down*". There was an idyllic holiday in the Conwy valley, but it was here that his foster-parents had to tell him that his mother had died in Guernsey.

Most of the Guernsey evacuees who have supplied their memories were happy in Neston and very grateful to their foster-families. Inevitably there were some exceptions. One girl could not get on with the son of the family and was moved to a more successful billet. Charlie Le Prevost spent only three months in Neston and did not like it:

This period of time was not always a happy one. We [Charles and his cousin Walter Fallaize] *were made to help dig an air raid shelter, bath in cold water, and many other things the rest of the family did not have to do.*

This experience echoes that of a Guernsey boy called Eric who, with his brother, was billeted in Irby. Their foster-mother fed and cared for them properly, but she would not let them play after school (although her son could), and made them work hard at gardening and housework.

Clothes could be a problem for the evacuees. "*The Red Cross was extremely good in clothing us in serviceable clothes.*" These clothes came from a depot in Stockport, but one girl found that only boys' shoes, socks and overcoat came in sizes suitable for her. "*How I hated wearing them!*" Charlie Le Prevost was in even worse plight, because his clothes were rapidly wearing out. He was told at school, almost daily, that if his foster-parents took him to the WVS, they would equip him with some decent clothes, but this never happened. Charlie's parents had also reached England and eventually traced him. When his mother came to fetch him from Neston, his only serviceable garment was his overcoat. By contrast, one girl remembered, "*One Christmas I received two new dresses. I was so excited to have something pretty, not realizing that the family had given clothes coupons for me.*"

Some of the Guernsey girls seem to have created a great impression with the local boys. Roy Booth knew one, Cynthia Hyams, who was billeted near his home. "*We lads were fascinated by Cynthia, and hung around her house in the hope of speaking to her, but she kept herself to herself.*" Colin Foote recalled, "*There were two young Guernsey teachers with French names who stayed somewhere in Little Neston. They were beautiful. Someone taught us to say 'Bonjour, mam'selle', to greet them as they passed by. Boyish hearts a-flutter!*" A less susceptible adult, however, thought them "*lazy — thought they were to be waited on*".

However much care and affection the foster-parents gave, the children were still separated from their own parents. "*It was our teachers, acting in loco parentis, who filled so many gaps and helped us to make the most of our five-year exile.*"

At long last the great day came when the children, some now young adults, could return to Guernsey. Some returned on 8 August, but others had to wait a little longer:

> *By August 1945 we were told to be ready to leave at any time. Two of my sisters from Bolton had special permission to travel back with the school. But it was September before we actually left. I was again excited to be travelling till I looked through the window and we said goodbye and Mrs Evans was crying. You see, they had been careful not to show too much love, knowing we would have to part, but when I saw the tears I wanted to get out. We went to Weymouth, then on the boat, and we were all on deck as we approached Guernsey. Cousins were there to meet us in their car and took us to Mum. Who was this very thin, stern-looking lady and two more sisters? My mother's first thought was how much we had all grown and how pale we were. I cried for a week, wanting to come back to Neston, but then settled down, once again having to get used to new friends.*

Not all the evacuees returned to the Channel Islands at once. Burnice Priaulx was to remain in Neston until 1952, and Ruby Le Ruez worked in her foster-father's paint shop and remained in Neston. The teacher, Ada Torode, went to teach at the 'top school' in Liverpool Road in 1944. She returned to Guernsey in 1946 but came back to this area, teaching first in Thornton Hough, then from 1963 to 1969 as deputy head of the new primary school in Raby Park Road, and finally at Greasby infants' school as head.

Most of those who have contributed their memories are deeply grateful for the love and care they were shown, and many lifelong friendships were formed. *"I will never forget my second family and how much kindness they showed me. Neston, we thank you!"* And the Lieutenant Governor of Guernsey wrote to Neston Council in December 1946 *"with very great gratitude"*.

In March 1941 a German bomber dropped two parachute mines in the Mersey off Rock Ferry, near to HMS *Conway*, a training ship for cadets. This ship was not damaged, but a nearby freighter loaded with steel, the *Tacoma City*, was sunk. The cadets from the *Conway*, numbering about two hundred, *"were told to lash up in their hammocks a plate, cutlery and sports gear, and proceed to the station with all speed"*. It had been arranged that they should find temporary refuge in Parkgate at Mostyn House, although the school was full with its usual complement of boys and staff. The lucky cadets got a bed, and as for the rest:

> *On arrival we were dispersed about the school, a number of us setting our hammocks on the gymnasium floor, the boys from the school sleeping in the underground air raid shelter. Despite watchful eyes, quite a few cadets managed to slip out at night and visit the local hostelry, others letting them back in on their return.*

After a few days the cadets were sent home and the *Conway* was towed to a safer mooring in the Menai Straits, Anglesey.

It was not just children and families who sought refuge in Neston. Several commercial firms also moved here or set up offices here. J. J. Walsh Ltd, wholesale wine and spirit merchants, relocated from Atherton Street, Liverpool, and set up a 'temporary wartime address' at the far end of Hinderton Road. Marcus H. Barlow & Co., hardware merchants from St Anne Street, Liverpool, set up in the Oddfellows Hall at Ness. United Molasses, which had several premises in Liverpool, also established themselves at Overdale, Hinderton Road. Tranmere Laundry, of Dial Road, Birkenhead, took over the Neston and Parkgate Laundry in Old Quay Lane. Leeman's Printers, from Water Street, Liverpool, came to West Vale in Little Neston because Jack Leeman himself already lived here, in Mellock Lane. Later this firm was to move to Leighton Road. Victor Horsman moved his motorcycle works from Liverpool to Leighton Road early in 1941 to set up a precision engineering workshop making war supplies. A firm which was set up in Cross Street, National Economy Salvage Fuels (oil reclamation), also arrived during the war and was probably an evacuee. This firm advertised a range of oil stoves with such names as 'Victory V', which ran on their own fuel, called NOCO. An unusual set of refugees were the antique pianos and organs which Rushworth & Dreaper, the Liverpool music firm, stored at Parkgate in May 1940, in two rooms rented from Daryl Grenfell. Some of the paintings from Liverpool's Walker Art Gallery were removed to Leahurst, the house on the Chester High Road which the University of Liverpool developed as a veterinary field station in 1941.

The turmoil in Europe, and in particular Hitler's murderous hatred of Jews, caused an influx of refugees, a few of whom came to Neston. In November 1938 a conference at Riverside, Manorial Road, Parkgate was addressed by Sir John Hope-Simpson, chairman of the Christian Council for Refugees from Germany and Central Europe. As a result a Wirral Refugee Committee was formed and issued an appeal, addressed from Riverside (the home of Margaret Corke and Annie Gibbs), for hospitality and funds. One result of this appeal was a letter from the Leverhulme estate office at Thornton Hough, asking farmers to provide board, lodging and agricultural training for refugee boys aged 14 to 17. One such refugee was Karl Jennings, who came to England from Vienna. After training he became farm manager at Ashfield Hall Farm, owned by Joe Johnson, a potato and produce merchant. And a family called Netch had to flee from Czechoslovakia, but became separated, and one of the daughters, Marie, came to Parkgate. When her parents and two brothers arrived, they all lived at Riverside, and eventually went to Canada.

Those evacuees who went overseas, mostly to Canada, were known as 'seavacuees'. One of those who considered this escape route was Daryl Grenfell, headmaster of Mostyn House, whose own children had been offered refuge, rather impractically, in the United States by his famous but elderly uncle, Sir Wilfred Grenfell. Many boarding schools, for whom parental confidence was everything, removed themselves to remote rural locations as soon as war seemed likely. The other two boarding schools in Wirral did so: The Leas School at Hoylake moved to the Lake District (Glenridding on Ullswater); Moorland House in Heswall moved to Chirk, and its buildings were requisitioned for Wallasey evacuees. In September 1938 Daryl Grenfell laid plans to move the whole school to the Waterloo Hotel at Betws-y-Coed. In giving permission for his son to go, one parent wrote, *"May I sincerely congratulate and thank you for your thoughtful foresight. While preparing for the worst we still hope and pray for the best."* But the Betws-y-Coed plan proved impracticable, and in the spring of 1939 Grenfell began building a very large air raid shelter. In August he wrote to parents, *"I am now convinced we will be far better off here than in North Wales, whither I had planned to go in the last crisis."*

But in June 1940, when a German invasion seemed all too likely, Grenfell began making enquiries about the possibility of moving the school, as a unit, to Canada. He enlisted the help of Lord Leverhulme (an Old Boy of the school) and Sir John Shute, MP. Leverhulme reported that the Canadian Government would welcome such a move, and Canada House would *"take the matter up energetically"* if a definite proposal were made.

Three members of the Netch family, refugees from Czechoslovakia, who stayed in Parkgate before before moving on to Canada.

Sir John Shute tracked down his parliamentary colleague Geoffrey Shakespeare (Under-Secretary of State, Dominions Office), who made two points: shipping space was limited and many were seeking to emigrate; and how could the project be financed when the British Government would not allow the expenditure of dollars? Shute added,

I must also tell you frankly that he did give me to understand that the Government generally was not desirous of panic transference, and especially boys of good standing, who he thought should be guided towards staying in the country of their birth at a critical period of its history rather than seeking a way out of it. Shakespeare told the House of Commons that, 'Such a policy [of permitting whole schools to emigrate] would militate against the spirit of resolution and tenacity with which we intend to prosecute the war.'

A. M. D. Grenfell, headmaster of Mostyn House School, was assiduous in maintaining the safety and wellbeing of his pupils.

Meanwhile, parents were asked if they would agree for their boys to go to Canada with the school. Out of about 130, 70 said they would agree, some wanting their daughters to be included. But in July Grenfell wrote to parents that the scheme was considered by the Government to be unnecessary and undesirable. He reported

the quiet and cheerful confidence of the authorities in our ability to keep this country a great deal safer than pessimistic imagination would portray. The undoubted dangers attached to the sea voyage seem to compare unfavourably with those of remaining here.

These dangers were very real. On 17 September 1940 the *City of Benares* was sunk with 73 seavacuees on board.

Grenfell then leased a farmhouse with twelve bedrooms in North Wales at Cerrigydrudion, and made it available in the holidays to any parents who wished to send their children there. In May 1941 he advised parents that if Mostyn House became unusable for any reason, like an unexploded bomb, the school would evacuate to Cerrigydrudion. Detailed plans were made to send the pupils first to Neston Laundry in Old Quay Lane and thence into Wales by bus or train. Thirty could sleep at the farmhouse and the rest in local hotels and billets in the village.

There were few air attacks on Merseyside after May 1941, but there was a 'little blitz' on London in the first four months of 1944, followed by the flying bombs or V-rockets — the V-1s, or Doodlebugs, from June to September, and the V-2s, much more fearsome because they travelled faster than sound, from September to December. All this caused a further wave of evacuation from London. On 31 July 1944 Neston received a party of evacuees from London, specifically from West Harrow. They were assembled in the parish church hall, where Dr Yeoman inspected them (one child had scarlet fever), and then they were billeted in Neston or Parkgate. Fifteen of them were admitted to the Liverpool Road school. At the end of September some complete families from London were housed in hostels at Clayhill, with more coming in October. Fifty-nine children from these families were admitted to the Liverpool Road school. In October the City of London Council wrote to Neston to give thanks for the way in which the evacuees were received. The remaining London evacuees were sent home in July 1945. It was not until December 1946 that the last child under the Government evacuation scheme had returned to Liverpool.

At least one child was evacuated away from Neston. In April 1941, when David Woodhouse was at home with his mother in Willaston, the dog came to his mother and whined. They then heard a tremendous thud at the back of the house. Three quarters of an hour later the dog whined again; there was a whistling sound and another thud. *"When father returned home he went into the garden and came back with the fin of a bomb. There was a big hole in the ground with an unexploded 500 lb. bomb in it, and another bomb beside the hedge."* David was sent to his grandparents in Herefordshire for six months.

SOURCES

This chapter was written by Geoffrey Place. Information from the files of Neston Urban District Council was researched by Susan Chambers.

We are very grateful to the following residents of Guernsey: Marion Batiste (née Tostevin), who was billeted with Mr and Mrs Evans; Burnice Dorey (née Priaulx), who lived with Mr and Mrs Buglass; Enid Le Cras and Phyllis Sarre (née Brehault), who lived with Mary and Tom Abel; Charlie Le Prevost; Nancy Moore, who stayed with Mr and Mrs Dovey; Barbara Tostevin, who was billeted with Walter and Doris Moulsdale; Bob Tostevin, who lived with Elsie and Joe Jones; E. W., who stayed with Mrs Dora Moore; and E. W.'s husband Eric.

We are grateful for the memories of Joe Birkett, who lived with Mrs T. Brett, who received 21 evacuees altogether; Irene Cottrell, who was billeted with Mrs Hattie Hough; Dot McCabe (née Burrows), who stayed with Mr and Mrs Hughes; and Anne Millington, whose parents took in two Guernsey children and a boy from London.

We also thank Roy Booth, Kathleen Byrne, Doreen Chrimes, Mary Chrimes, Marie and Vincent Crook, Lettice Crossley, Colin Foote, Doris Gittos, Muriel Grantham, Anne Gray, Tommy Maddox, Andrew Prince, Betty Pritchard, Mary Sir (née Scarratt) and David Woodhouse for their memories.

D. N. Thompson, archivist at Birkenhead Central Library, supplied details from the minutes of Wallasey Education Committee. David Quaife, head teacher of Elleray Park School, kindly allowed access to the school's records. Julian Grenfell, headmaster of Mostyn House School, has allowed the use of material from the school's archives. Andrew Cubley gave information about HMS *Conway*, including quotations from John Masefield and Jim Thompson. Susan Chambers extracted details from the records of the Liverpool Road school.

CHAPTER THREE

AIRCRAFT OVER NESTON

The RAF expanded very rapidly during the war. In September 1939 its strength was 2,600 aircraft and 174,000 personnel. By May 1945 these numbers had risen to 9,200 operational aircraft and 1,079,835 personnel. A massive training programme took place to supply the aircrew to fly these extra aircraft. Training bases had to be situated as far as possible from enemy activity. Therefore many airfields were built in the North-West, and while none were in the Neston area, there were several nearby. Hooton Park and Sealand airfields originated in the First World War, but activity declined after 1918. The threat of war led to expansion in the late 1930s. In 1936 No.610 (County of Chester) Squadron was formed at Hooton. It was equipped with Hawker Hind biplane light bombers. Soon after the war started it was re-equipped with Spitfires and was sent south. Ansons and Tiger Moths were based there in the autumn of 1939. RAF training was also to expand at Sealand. In 1940 some Miles Master training aircraft were fitted with machine-guns, as there were few fighters to spare, to defend the North-West while the Battle of Britain was fought in the South-East.

Hawarden, to the south of Chester, was designed as a 'shadow' factory to produce Vickers-Armstrong Wellington bombers. (Shadow factories were set up in case the parent factories were bombed.) Some people from Neston worked in this factory on a variety of jobs. Little Sutton airfield opened in 1941 and was used by Tiger Moths of the Elementary Flying School. This was a small airfield and was closed soon after the war ended.

Local people would see aircraft from these bases flying over Neston. Schoolboys used to practise their aircraft recognition from cards showing the silhouettes of the different planes. Maurice Jones was at Ness Holt school during the war, and remembers that, on Saturday afternoons, he and a friend sat on the colliery waste tip and watched planes diving to drop bombs on the bombing range on the marshes opposite Burton. This was downstream of Burton Cop. Bombs dropped here formed flashes or pools on which wildfowl would settle. After the war the local wildfowlers called these pools the Bombing Target Flashes. *"We watched*

Chapter Three

The Vickers Supermarine Spitfire was a distinctive shape and sound in Britain's wartime skies, and is probably the aircraft most clearly remembered from those days.

Mosquitoes and Beaufighters and counted the time from the dive to when we saw the smoke bomb burst." He also saw a Tiger Moth in the field where the Woodfall Lane schools are now. *"It had run out of fuel and a petrol bowser came out, and I stood and watched while the pilot took off. A Hurricane landed in the field behind the reservoir in Lees Lane. It was intact and was on the ground for 48 hours, while the Home Guard looked after it."* Both these incidents were early in the war.

Defence planners had not made any significant provision for air defence in the North-West, as it was not thought necessary. But with the defeat of France in June 1940, the German air force, the *Luftwaffe*, could use bases in north-west France to attack Liverpool. Initially there were a number of daylight reconnaissance missions. Eddie Scott who lived in Little Neston remembered,

> *One sunny evening while sitting at the piano beside a window, I was startled by the sudden deafening noise of an aircraft engine, and a plane flashed directly overhead, scarcely above rooftop level. I still vividly remember the sense of shock with which I recognized the black crosses on its wings, and my relief when I realized it hadn't dropped anything.*

Arnold Whiteway went wildfowling in a punt mounted with a gun:

> *I was in the middle of the river and a German plane about 1,000 feet up went towards Summers'* [the steelworks at Shotton]. *Nothing fired at it. I looked at the shape of the punt and thought, I hope he doesn't think we are a submarine and attack us.*

On 14 August 1940 a Heinkel He111P bombed Sealand, but soon afterwards was intercepted by three Spitfires from Hawarden. The Heinkel crash-landed at Border House Farm on the outskirts of Chester.

Many local people saw a British Hurricane fighter attack a German Dornier Do17Z-3 at about 6.30 in the evening of 11 October 1940. The Dornier crashed into the Dee estuary off West Kirby, and the aircraft and its crew were never located. Miss Barber remembered,

> We heard machine-guns. Jessie Durham and I ran down the garden path as far as we could. We shouted at the top of our voices, 'He's got him!' The planes came over the houses and seemed to be coming from Liverpool. They were flying in a line parallel to Hinderton Road towards Wales. They were well up in the air and we could see the flashes of the guns. It was obvious who was chasing whom.

One German plane, which crashed elsewhere, caused a sensation when it was put on show at Parkgate. On 8 October 1940 a Junkers 88 was intercepted by three Hurricanes from 312 Squadron based at Speke. It made a belly landing near Bromborough Dock in Port Sunlight. It had a crew of four, of whom one was killed, one wounded and two were unharmed prisoners. The RAF report on the incident said, *"There were about fifty .303 bullet strikes, about six of which were in the starboard engine."* The plane was exhibited at several sites around Wirral, including the Oval at Bebington and off Bevyl Road at Parkgate. The *Birkenhead Advertiser* for 16 November 1940 stated,

> GERMAN BOMBER AT PARKGATE Mrs Anstead-Browne of the WVS, and local organizer of the Neston Spitfire Fund, has secured a Junkers 88 as a means of receiving revenue for her effort. This is now on view on a field adjoining the Parade at Parkgate, where it is to remain till November 24th. A charge of 6d. per adult and 3d. for children is being made, and already a large number of people have looked at the machine.

Arthur Draper, who was eight years old at the time, remembers the Junkers came on low loaders, the fuselage on one and the wings on the other. They placed it together so that it looked as though it had belly-flopped. *"I took a bit of the tail fin which was lying on the ground. It was dark green and smelled like rotten cheese. I put it in our shed but my dad made me throw it away as it had such a terrible smell."* Quite a number of those who came to see this plane thought it had come down at Parkgate.

Local boys were very keen to collect souvenirs, and so the plane was guarded at night by the Home Guard. Eddie Scott remembers,

The Little Neston company of the Home Guard was charged with the responsibility for protecting it from the depredations of souvenir-hunters. The half-dozen of us detailed for the task made our way to the rendezvous, an empty house behind what is now the Parkgate Hotel, and mounted a patrolling guard in pairs for the standard two hours on and four off. I remember the four off particularly for the hardness of the bare floor and the inadequacy of the single blanket, and the two on for the inky blackness of the night.

Maurice Jones went to see the plane:

There were plenty of people there and it poured with rain. It was a very miserable day. Corrugated sheets had been put on the ground round the plane as it was so wet. A wing had come off the plane but was laid out as it should have been. There was a long line of people waiting to go in, and you went in through the door the crew had used. It was the first German object of war I had ever seen. I went in and sat in the pilot's seat and I can remember a lady saying they needed terribly long legs to reach the pedals.

During the Battle of Britain the *Luftwaffe* started bombing at night. Fighter Command was ill prepared for a night war. The main German effort was to bomb London, but from late July 1940 several major attacks were launched against Liverpool. The RAF had to meet this threat, but it found Hurricanes and Spitfires were ineffective and expensive in casualties for night use in blackout conditions, without VHF radios. Therefore, Defiant two-seater fighters were used to fill the gap in the air defences. This aircraft had been withdrawn from daylight sorties as the loss rate had been very high. It had four .303 Browning machine-guns mounted in a turret behind the pilot and operated by a second crew member. It had a wide undercarriage which made night landings simpler. Pilots would approach from below and the gunners were able to shoot almost vertically upwards. It took time to get the Defiant squadrons ready, and it was not until the spring of 1941 that they were fully operational. Defiants and some Hurricanes were based at Cranage, near Holmes Chapel, and at Squires Gate near Blackpool. Both these airfields were well distant from Liverpool, and this added to the difficulty of defending the city.

The most dramatic events remembered by the people of Neston were those occasions when enemy aircrew baled out and were taken prisoner. Three German planes were hit over the Dee during the fiercest attacks on Liverpool, the main port for the receipt of supplies from America, during March and May 1941. On the night of 12/13 March over 300 German bombers attacked Merseyside, dropping 303 tons of high explosive and

64,152 incendiaries. To meet them, 178 British night-fighters were sent up. The next morning Annie Johnson wrote this letter:

> We had a terrible raid during the night — not here but on Merseyside, and you know what that means. It started at 8.30 last night and went on in a most savage manner until 4 a.m. We watched the display of 'fireworks' and what we have since been told were two dogfights in the sky. I have just heard that a bomber was brought down at Parkgate and they have the German airmen at the police station. If it is so and they can salvage the plane, it will be the very thing they were wanting for the War Weapons Week on the 25th. Harold Gill took the two fellows prisoner — they gave up their revolvers without any to-do and one could speak English — only 23 — and he said he was glad to be out of it all. Two more of them were captured Heswall or Thurstaston way — they all came down by parachute and one at Neston police station has the Iron Cross and Bar.

Some of the Bushell family were watching in Parkgate: "The pilot baled out and we watched him walk to the shore from about halfway out. He came to the Watch House door and gave himself up. Mum made him a cup of tea and Dad took him to Harold Gill who was in the Home Guard." Harold Gill, who lived at The Warren on the Parkgate Parade, had been a conscientious objector during the First World War. That did not stop him, on this occasion, from herding his captives with a shotgun. Miss Johnson was wrongly informed that a plane came down at Parkgate, but she was right about the two dogfights. Of the seven German aircrew who baled out, we do not know which two were held at Neston. Andrew Prince saw them when on ARP duty at Neston police station. "I looked through the window in the cell door and I remember thinking how young they looked, and how wretched were their uniforms. Their footwear was very poor."

In the descriptions of German planes which follow, KG indicates *Kampfgruppe*, the Battle Group to which they belonged.

One dogfight was between a Heinkel and a Hurricane. The Heinkel 111P-4 (works number 2989 from 6-KG55) was over Liverpool when it was spotted by Sgt McNair flying a Hurricane of 96 Squadron from Cranage. He saw the Heinkel against the glare of fires in Liverpool at 12,000 feet and made three attacks. The stricken aircraft was tracked by the Royal Observer Corps and was seen flying down the Dee from the direction of Hilbre. Members of the crew were seen to bale out: W. Berlin, K. Single and X. Diem baled out and were captured; L. Kutznik and H. Ludwinski were killed. The aircraft, code GI-OP, crashed at 22.10 hours on the ICI recreation ground at Widnes and was destroyed.

Chapter Three

CROSVILLE

MESSAGE FOR WAR WEAPONS WEEK

SAVE OR SLAVE

How do you intend to TRAVEL . . . through the "HAPPY VALLEY OF THRIFT" to victory and peace . . . or along the grim "ROAD OF INDIFFERENCE" to tyranny and humiliation? . . . It is for you to decide right now which of these two ROUTES it is to be . . . But have no doubt, no hesitation . . . This is to be an historic TRIP . . . With our fighting forces DRIVING and Mr. Churchill CONDUCTING . . . the VEHICLE of our destinies is in most capable and confident hands . . . so HURRY along, please . . . plenty of ROOM on TOP . . . and let us get away to a rousing START . . . The JOURNEY may be STEEP, but we shall continue to CLIMB up and up to the summit of achievement . . . and then we shall see the pleasing spectacle of a British COUNTRYSIDE rejoicing once more in peace and contentment.

J.G.G.

FARE

ANY VALUE IN WAR SAVINGS STAMPS - CERTIFICATES or BONDS

Issued by
Crosville Motor Services Ltd., Publicity Dept., Crane Wharf, Chester

Local companies played their part in encouraging the public to save. This advertisement was for War Weapons Week in April 1941.

The second dogfight was between a Junkers and a Defiant. The Junkers 88A-5 (works number 7188, from 9-KG76) was engaged by anti-aircraft fire over Birkenhead and the plane was chased by Sgt Jankowiak in a Defiant of 307 Squadron towards Chester. The aircraft was hit several times and was seen to be on fire and losing height rapidly. It turned north-west and members of the crew were seen to bale out. Their names were G. Unger, F. Bergman, A. Meier and W. Dirk, all of whom were arrested when they landed. Gunther Unger later wrote in his diary,

> *I looked round and saw a small but very bright glow on the cowling behind the starboard engine. The metal was actually burning, which meant the heat must have been intense, probably a fire within the engine nacelle. At first the visible spot of fire was very small, but it grew rapidly and flames began to trail behind the aircraft. I could see there was no hope of getting home, so I ordered the crew to bale out. The flight engineer opened the escape hatch at the rear and jumped, followed by the radio operator. After they left I trimmed the aircraft until it was pointing towards the sea, so that when it crashed there would be nothing for the enemy to find. As I left my seat the observer dropped out of the hatch. The Junkers was flying properly trimmed, straight and level, perfectly well on both engines. For a moment I considered trying to get home alone but a further glance at the blaze made it clear this would not be possible. I clambered to the rear and followed my crew out of the hatch.*

What happened to this aircraft was not solved until 1978, when investigators discovered that the aircraft had turned round and flown on, eventually crashing into trees and houses at The Croft, Wychbold, in Worcestershire.

A month later, the third German plane to be abandoned by its crew over the Dee was a Heinkel 111P-4 (works number 2874, from 3-KG55). This aircraft left Le Bourget airfield in northern France and followed the route Lands End, St David's Head, Holyhead and Liverpool. It followed pathfinders to attack Liverpool docks. The crew were Heinz Dunkerbeck (pilot), Fritz Kitzing (observer), Joachim Salm (wireless operator) and Cornell Mildenbirger (flight mechanic and gunner). The plane dropped its bombs and turned south. It was attacked by a Defiant night-fighter from 256 Squadron based at Squires Gate, Blackpool. The Defiant's pilot was Flying Officer D. Toone and the gunner was Flying Officer R. L. Lamb. The gunfire from the Defiant was deadly accurate and killed the airmen behind the pilot and observer. The Defiant made two more attacks. The surviving crew baled out at 01.40 hours on 8 May 1941. The

Chapter Three

observer, Fritz Kitzing, landed on the Welsh side of the Dee near Flint, and the pilot at Parkgate. Cyril Cambridge was there:

> *I was in the Little Neston Home Guard hut. I was off duty and had gone out because there was a heavy raid, and I was standing chatting to other residents when we heard a guttural voice behind us. We then saw a German coming up the slope by the Boat House Café and he gave himself up to us. The man was clean and tidy in his uniform.*

Leslie Jervis recalled, "We tried to communicate with signs. After a few minutes some Army people came along and we handed the airman over to them." The soldiers were a patrol led by 2nd Lieut. K. C. Addy, of Z Company, 9th Battalion of the Royal Northumberland Fusiliers. The unit's war diary records that they captured *Leutnant* Heinz Dunkerbeck.

William Brown, who served in the battalion at the time, remembers, "He was brought to our guard room at Leighton School. Our prisoner was collected by the military police later in the night and would eventually go to a prisoner-of-war camp."

The RAF moved fast to improve its night-fighter capabilities. The first serious adversary for the night-bomber was the Bristol Beaufighter. It was a twin-engined fighter with a top speed of 330 m.p.h. and armed with 20 mm cannon instead of machine-guns. Jeremy Howard-Williams was undertaking elementary flying training on Tiger Moths at Sealand in the spring of 1941. He wrote. "*On the far side of the airfield black Beaufighters*

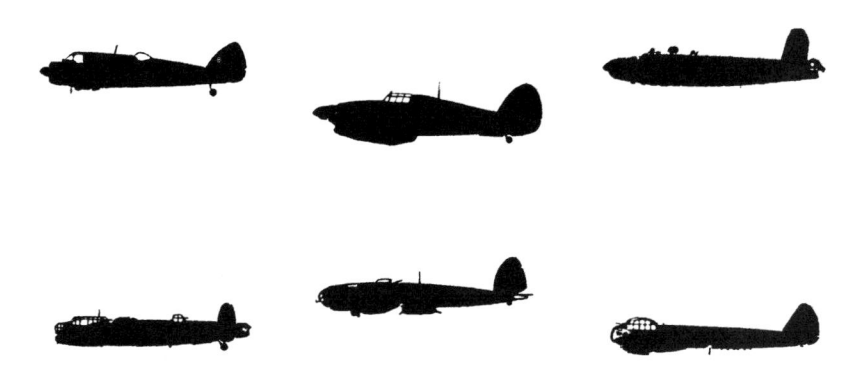

Us and them. These were some of the aircraft seen over Neston and the surrounding district. *L. to r: top*, Bristol Beaufighter, Hawker Hurricane, Vickers Wellington; *bottom*, Avro Lancaster, Heinkel He111, Junkers Ju88 (not to scale).

were being wheeled in and out of a hangar for a most secret modification about which nobody was allowed to speak." This modification was the fitting of airborne interception radar as it was delivered from the manufacturers.

Although a number of German planes flew over Neston, none actually came down in this area. There were a considerable number of British planes, however, which crashed hereabouts. This is not surprising, bearing in mind that many incidents concerned training aircraft. Records have been found of twelve British aircraft which crashed in the Neston area.

On 1 July 1941 a Tiger Moth (T7156) from 19 Elementary Flying Training School (EFTS), Sealand, landed at Woodcroft Farm, Willaston. The official report said the pilot was making a practice forced landing when the engine failed to pick up as the throttle opened after gliding down. The pilot sideslipped to avoid high tension cables and the wing hit the ground. Thelma Hale, a child at the time, saw the plane burst into flames. The pilot rolled out and was helped to the farmhouse by the district nurse, Nurse Lloyd, and a farm worker, Tom Higginson. The accident was deemed to be caused by the inexperience of the pilot. Another Tiger Moth (R4902) from Sealand also crashed near Neston on the same day.

On 15 April 1942 a Hurricane (V6843) from the Merchant Ship Fighter Unit, RAF Speke, and a Tiger Moth (T7298) from 24 EFTS Sealand, collided in mid-air near Parkgate, both pilots being killed. On 14 August 1942 Tiger Moth DE726 from 24 EFTS Sealand made a forced landing at Raby Farm, Willaston, because of engine failure. The plane overturned but the pilot was unhurt.

There is more local information about the crash of Tiger Moth R5077 in Burton on 10 September 1941. It was from the Merchant Ship Fighter Unit, RAF Speke. The official report said there was unauthorized low flying when the plane was caught in a violent air current and was unable to recover from the subsequent spin. Pilot Officer A. V. Saunders and his non-RAF passenger were injured. Mrs Jill Pratt (née Latham) lived at Mercia, Vicarage Lane, Burton, and she saw the Tiger Moth come down. *"I saw the pilots tense themselves and I thought it would hit the house, but it landed in the garden."* Her brother Frank Latham remembered,

> We had a long lawn at Mercia which my father was mowing. He turned at the end and was somewhat surprised to find a Tiger Moth had crash-landed at the other end. The crew of two were taken to Clatterbridge Hospital and recovered. My first duty in Burton Home Guard was to stand sentry over the crashed plane in my own garden.

Chapter Three

There were several crashes on the marshes. On 18 August 1941 Spitfire R6957 from 57 Operational Training Unit, Hawarden, belly-landed on Burton marsh because of engine failure. It did not have sufficient height to get to Sealand, but the pilot was uninjured. On 8 January 1943 a Blackburn Botha (wireless operator trainer), L6287 from 11 Radio School, Hooton Park, force-landed on Flint Bank. The crew were rescued the next day. The aircraft was not salvaged until about 1953, and was visible from Boathouse Lane in Parkgate.

A Wellington (T2475) from 21 Operational Training Unit, Moreton-in-Marsh, crashed on 24 August 1943 on the marshes not far from the Harp Inn. The port engine failed in flight and the pilot carried out an excellent forced landing. Two of the crew were injured. Some time later the aircraft was salvaged by the RAF. The wreckage was put on a low loader and taken up Marshlands Road. By the time they reached the top it was lunchtime, and the salvage crew parked the lorry at the side of the road and went to a local pub. While they were away local children swarmed over the plane, collecting parts as souvenirs. Pieces of Perspex were highly valued as they could be made into key rings.

An Avro Anson training aircraft landed in a field at the top of Woodfall Lane. Hugh Norman thought it was about 1943. He went there early one morning and was surprised to see three RAF men guarding it. The Anson was halfway through a hedge and it looked as though the landing gear had failed. Later it was taken away in pieces.

A crash which made a lasting impression on all who saw it was Mosquito HJ816 from 60 Operational Training Unit, RAF High Ercall, Shropshire. It crashed on 10 September 1944 during air-to-ground gunnery attacks on Burton marsh bombing range. The crew were killed. The pilot was Flying Officer Guy Merson Templer and the navigator was Flying Officer Derek Allan Attwood, both of the Royal New Zealand Air Force. They were buried in the war graves plot of Blacon cemetery. Local people thought they were Canadians because part of a greatcoat with a 'Canada' badge and other items were found at the crash site. Andrew Prince was the first on the scene:

> *The Mosquito crashed in a field in Ness off Snab Lane. I lived in West Vale and I heard the plane come over so low that I thought it might have hit the chimney. It was flying parallel to the railway line. I got out of bed, got the car out and drove there. The plane was on fire, ammunition was exploding and there was no one alive.*

Down in Neston 1939 –1945

Mosquito HX917 of No. 487 squadron, RNZAF, Hunsdon, July 1943 – Similar to the one that crashed at Ness in 1944.

Although Neston did not have an airfield within its boundaries during the Second World War there were several active bases in the vicinity (i.e. Hawarden, Hooton, Sealand, Speke and Little Sutton). No German planes actually landed but several enemy airmen parachuted to safety and were captured in the Neston District after being shot down whilst raiding Liverpool.

However, a dozen allied aircraft came to grief in the area during this period. A recent publication, "Neston at War 1939-1945", compiled by the Burton and Neston History Society outlines the details of these incidents.

Most of the early incidents involved Tiger Moths. Two from No 19 Elementary Flying School at Sealand crashed on the same day (1st July 1941) in separate accidents at Willaston and Neston. On the 15th April 1942, another Sealand-based Moth collided in mid-air over Parkgate with a Hurricane from the Merchant Ship Fighter Unit at Speke with the loss of both pilots. Other Moths from Sealand and Speke also crashed but without fatalities at Burton in September 1941 and at Willaston in August 1942. Causes of the crashes were attributed to pilot error, engine failure and unauthorised low flying.

Several aircraft came down in Burton Marshes over the course of the war. A Spitfire from No. 57 OTU at Hawarden belly-landed on 18th August 1942 because of engine-failure. This was followed in January 1943 by a Blackburn Botha from 11 Radio School at Hooton Park that force-landed on Flint Bank. The crew were rescued but the airframe remained unsalvaged until 1953. Later that year, a Wellington from 21 OTU at Moreton-in-Marsh crashed near The Harp Inn. The plane's port engine failed and the pilot force-landed. Two crewmen were injured but there were no fatalities.

Jetstream Club volunteers pose next to the aircraft at the Marriott Hotel

The process of dismantling of the aircraft commenced on January 25th at Woodford. Shortly after, the airframe components were transferred to Speke, unloaded and reassembled. A schedule of regular maintenance will be compiled and undertaken. It is possible that "Open Days" will be held when visitors will be able to view the aircraft for a nominal charge to help with costs. It is even envisaged that the aircraft could be used for business meetings or as a temporary classroom for schoolchildren who wish to learn about aviation.

It promises to be an interesting and exciting addition to the aviation heritage of Merseyside. The sight of another airframe at the old airport terminal at Speke as well as the Dragon Rapide replica should be welcomed. All Merseyside aviation enthusiasts are invited to join the Jetstream Club and work on the aircraft on a regular or occasional basis. Initial joining fee is only £15 per annum but other costs may be incurred if or when required. This sum includes membership identification badge, overalls and protective headgear. There is also Associate Membership available for £5 per annum for those who wish to support the project or visit the aircraft on site. It is proposed to produce a regular newsletter that will update members on progress and set up a website that will include photographs.

For further details please contact Malcolm Kinnear, the Chairman of the Jetstream Club, on 0151 645 5704.

Maurice Jones also heard the plane:

> *I was in bed and the plane made several passes over Little Neston. It was so low you could not miss it. When we got to school the next morning we were all questioned by a policeman who asked if we had seen anything. Later on we all trooped down there. The plane was still smouldering, there was a hole in the ground and an awful smell.*

Bill Jones also went to the site:

> *When I arrived at the crash, which was a few yards on the river side of Well Lane railway bridge, there was just the smouldering remains of the plane, but more sad and horrifying were the bits and pieces of those poor souls' bodies.*

Some aircraft could land and take off in a very short distance. Such an aircraft was the Fairey Swordfish biplane, which was used by the Royal Navy as a torpedo bomber on its aircraft carriers. One day Andrew Prince was very surprised to see one of these aircraft in a field off West Vale, which then stretched a few hundred yards beyond the railway bridge.

> *I went home and a Fairey Swordfish had landed in Bob Scott's field. I went over to the plane and the pilot asked, 'Where is the nearest aerodrome?' I told him it was Sealand. 'You just follow the railway line and you cannot miss it.' The pilot said, 'By God I can! Can I take off on this field?' I said, 'There are undulations in the field so watch out and try to avoid the colliery spoil heaps.' I said I would advise the police to phone Sealand to put the lights on as it was getting dark.*

One crash occurred just after the war ended, on 16 November 1945. The pilot, Walter Swain, was flying an Airspeed Oxford when his wireless failed and he could not find his way in bad weather. As his fuel was running out, he decided to bale out. Mrs Reece (née McMaster) lived at a farm in The Runnel near Parkgate. She heard the plane coming down and heard it crash.

> *Mr Hook from next door and I went to look; we had no torch and it was pitch dark. We followed the bits of the plane on the ground and finally came across what was left in a tree. There was no one in it so we searched to see if the pilot had limped off. We went back home and phoned the police and ten minutes later they rang back to say the pilot had been found and was at a farmhouse having a cup of tea.*

The circumstances remained a mystery for fifty years; then the pilot revisited the scene of his parachute landing. He was said to have been the only person at that time to have survived baling out of an Airspeed Oxford.

Chapter Three

SOURCES

This chapter was written by Edward Hilditch.

Official records used included the report, *Location of Enemy Aircraft Brought Down in the UK, August–December 1940*, and the War Diary of the 9th Battalion, Royal Northumberland Fusiliers, both in the Public Record Office, Kew.

Other written sources were Jeremy Howard-Williams, *Night Intruder* (Air Life Publishing, 1992); Robin McNair, short article in *Air Pictorial*, aviation archaeology section, December 1997; and for background information, Norman Frank, *RAF Fighter Command* (Patrick Stephens, 1992).

The information on German aircraft and RAF crashes was provided by Steve Parsons and the museum of the Griffin Trust at Hooton.

We are also grateful for the memories of Joyce Barber, William Brown, Cyril Cambridge, Arthur Draper, Leslie Jervis, Annie Johnson, Bill Jones, Maurice Jones, Thelma Kameen (née Hale), Frank Latham, Hugh Norman, Jill Pratt, Mrs Reece, Eddie Scott, Walter Swain, Gunther Unger and Arnold Whiteway.

CHAPTER FOUR

AIR RAIDS

The first warning of attacking bombers was the air raid siren. These machines were operated electrically by the police and could be heard for miles. The warning sound undulated between two notes, which gave it the nickname 'Moaning Minnie', while the 'all-clear' was a single note; each lasted for two minutes. In Neston the siren was first mounted on the town hall but soon moved to the police station for ease of manning. There was a siren on top of Mostyn House School in Parkgate, on Burton Manor, on the War Memorial Hut in Willaston, at the Manor in Thornton Hough and for Raby there was a siren mounted on a pole in Blakeley Road. There were also three sirens in Heswall. Most of these were to stay in place, regularly tested by the police, for fifty years until the Cold War was seen to be over. The first air raid warning heard in Neston was on 17 November 1939 at 11.30 a.m., with the all-clear sounding two minutes later. The sirens did not always give adequate warning, and N. C. H. Tomlinson has written of raids on Birkenhead when he heard the drone of German aircraft engines before he heard the siren.

There were four types of aerial missile which were likely to land in the Neston area, three of them German. There were the high-explosive bombs, mostly of 50, 250 and 500 kilograms, which were designed to penetrate buildings or ships and blow them up. Only a few landed in Neston and its locality, where they did little damage apart from killing eleven cows in Raby. More common were incendiaries designed to start fires, mostly 1 kg and dropped in clusters. These had a thermite core and a magnesium case, both of which burned fiercely. Some of these did some damage at Parkgate, but most fell harmlessly in fields. A more fearsome weapon was the parachute mine. These were intended to land in the Mersey or its approaches to sink ships, but were often blown inland, where they could cause fearful damage. One of them caused the evacuation of HMS *Conway* cadets to Parkgate. One parachute mine exploded at Willaston and another at Puddington. The Willaston mine caused a mare to give birth prematurely, and the foal was named Blitz. The parachute of another caught in a tree at Raby House Farm, and the mine was defused by a bomb disposal squad.

During an air raid at Neston, the most likely cause of injury, as it fortunately turned out, was not from enemy bombs but from fragments of our own anti-aircraft shells. Neston Council actually warned people, in October 1940, that if they chose to leave their own homes during an air raid to go to a public shelter, *"it must be realized this is always dangerous through the possibility of falling shrapnel."* With gun batteries at Raby and Puddington, and mobile guns in a variety of places, the noise of the British response was often much greater than the noise of the raid itself. Showers of fragments littered the ground after every raid, and these could do damage. In November 1941 Daryl Grenfell was writing to the Ministry of Works about repairs to the roofs of Mostyn House School, damaged by shrapnel. He had earlier applied for a licence (which was refused) to buy wire mesh to protect his skylights. Wardens and other Civil Defence people had helmets for their protection, and members of the public were supposed, and could be ordered, to take cover during an air raid.

The first shelters were provided at the schools, and simple trenches were dug before war broke out. These became semi-underground structures with a concrete floor, steel frame and a curved roof of corrugated iron covered with earth and grass. At Burton Road,

> *an escape hatch through a vertical steel shaft with a steel ladder was provided at the opposite end to the door. A sort of conning tower with a space between the top of the steel lining and the hinged lid provided ventilation and the opportunity to view all round, no doubt to ensure all was clear if evacuation that way proved necessary. There was a row of slatted forms on either side and a third row in the middle.*

There were five shelters, each holding 40 people, for Liverpool Road school on the land behind the petrol station, and five of similar size at Ness Holt school. For Burton Road school there were eight shelters in the field on the opposite side of the road, holding 340 altogether. The children would file to their allotted shelters when the warning sounded and had to remain in that dark, musty-smelling atmosphere until the all-clear sounded. Fred (Tosh) Davies would read a story from the book, *Children of the New Forest*. Similar shelters were also built at the other schools in the district, but Parkgate infants' school had a brick shelter which caused a dispute in August 1940 when *"members of the public insist on the right to use the school's air raid shelter"*. This happened at other schools, and eventually the county council agreed that the public could use these shelters after school hours. However, the schools soon began to complain that candles and toilet paper were being stolen, clutter such as deck chairs were being left in them, locks had been smashed and there had been drunkenness and immoral behaviour.

By far the largest shelter in the district was built at Mostyn House School. Daryl Grenfell described it, in a letter to parents in July 1939, as

> *a very strong concrete box sunk into the ground. It is 100 feet long, 22 feet wide and 10 feet high. The walls are 24 inches thick, made of doubly reinforced waterproof concrete, the roof is supported by 19 steel girders spanned by corrugated steel sheets with doubly reinforced concrete right over the entire roof, on top of which is about three feet of clay which will be grassed.*

Ventilation was provided by fans at each end. Lighting was supplied by three independent units: the mains electricity, the school's own generator and a circuit from a large bus battery off a trickle-charger. The shelter was fitted with electric radiators, lavatories, wireless, telephone, external signal apparatus, emergency escape tools, first aid box, fire extinguisher, water and rations. Grenfell described his shelter to the ARP department of the Home Office, who replied,

> *Your shelter would hold 280 people without mechanical ventilation and 350 people with it, and would probably be of sufficient strength to withstand a direct hit from bombs of 50 lb. in weight.*

The shelter cost more than £2,500 to build. Grenfell paid for it partly by selling the Parkgate swimming baths and partly by appealing to parents for help. Originally the shelter was fitted with seats, which were adequate for daylight raids but not at night. In September 1940, when night-time raids seemed likely, Grenfell fitted bunks in the shelter, and delayed the start of term to 2 October until the bunks were ready. Parents were asked to provide Lilo mattresses and sleeping bags which would remain in the shelter. All the pupils had siren suits (rather like a modern tracksuit), and one pupil remembers that he had a furry one that made him look like a teddy bear. When the warning sounded at night, the school would be called, dormitory by dormitory, through a loudspeaker system in every room, putting on their siren suits and bringing a pillow. The whole building could be emptied in three minutes, and Mr Grenfell said that some children, on waking in their own beds in the morning, had not remembered that they had been down to the shelter, which they knew as 'the Dive'. When raids were expected, as in the 'May blitz' of 1941, the pupils would start the evening in the Dive and spend the whole night there.

The result of this provision was to boost parents' confidence in the school. Not only did Mostyn House not have to evacuate, but pupil numbers rose steadily throughout the war, from 124 in 1939 to 150 in 1945. Grenfell hoped that after the war a peaceful use could be found for the Dive, perhaps as an indoor cricket pitch, but it never proved very suitable for this or any other purpose, and was used chiefly as the point of assembly for fire drills. It is now used only for storage.

For the general public who might be caught in the streets by an alert, provision of shelters was much slower. Only one public trench shelter was built, at the junction of Badger Bait and Town Lane in Little Neston, which would hold 172 people. In October 1940 Neston Council met a Government requirement that an 'unspecified area' should have shelters for 7% of the population by strengthening the cellars of buildings. In Parkgate, both Balcony House and Sea View had massive timber frames built in their cellars, supposedly to support the building if it collapsed. The timbers in Sea View were left in place after the war in case their removal should disturb the building, but when the house was repaired in 1997 it was found that the framework was free-standing and it was safely removed. The cellars were provided with notices stating that they were public air raid shelters: that of Balcony House would take 55 people, and that of Sea View 85.

In Neston there were four such strengthened cellars: one was under the two shops at the Cross next to the church, Bradley's and Williams's, which would take 85 people. Another, which held 35, was under the ARP headquarters next to Jackson's tower; another was under Scott's in Bridge Street, since demolished; and there was one at Mrs Birch's, at 2 High Street. In Willaston there were four, including the Midland Bank. Ness had one at the shop and Burton one at Stanley House. Some of these cellars were entered through trapdoors, which people did not like because they felt trapped.

In 1940, when bombing became more widespread and indiscriminate, the Government increased the requirement for shelters in unspecified areas to 40%, and the council began building eight brick shelters. These were designed to accommodate 48 people each, and were provided behind Stone House in Burton; at New Street in Little Neston; two in Talbot Avenue and two in Mayfield Gardens; and one each in Brookland Road, Parkgate, and Mill Lane, Ness. These brick shelters were being built in the autumn of 1941, by which time the danger from bombers in this area was virtually over.

Chemical toilets were provided in the public shelters, but these needed caustic soda, which was dangerous stuff to handle as it could burn clothes and boots, as well as skin. Those who used it were advised to wear their gas masks if the fumes irritated their throats.

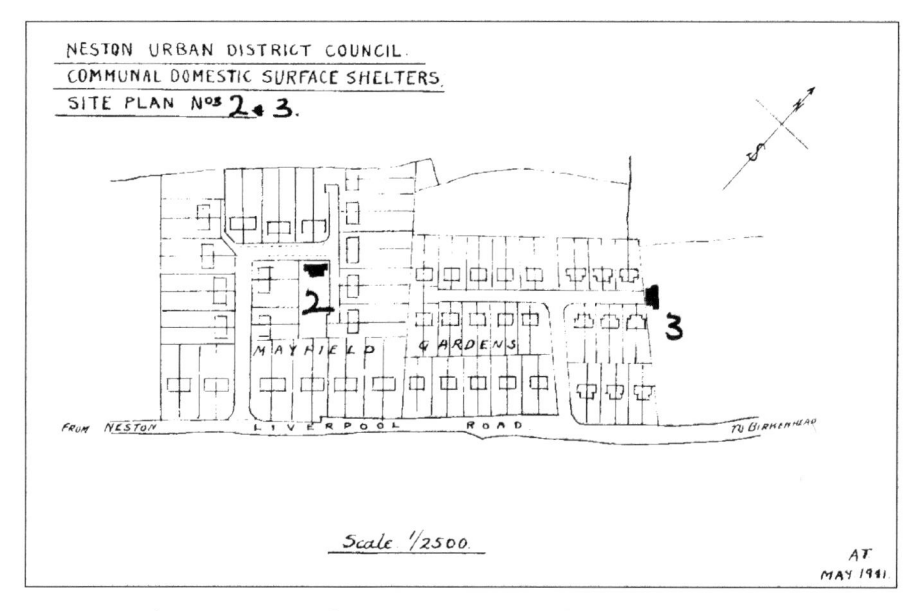

Eight brick air raid shelters were built for the public in the Neston urban district. Mayfield Gardens had two of them.

Householders were urged to take their own precautions against air raids, and many people never went to a public shelter. One solution was to make a 'safe room', or refuge, in your house:

> *Dad [Harry Foote] considered the living room to be the strongest part of the house and he had erected a timber and heavy-duty corrugated iron shutter over the window. This was closed at night to serve both as blackout and blast protection. It had quite a few pieces of shrapnel embedded in it when we eventually took it down. In due course after the war it became the roof of my motorbike garage.*

> *All windows were covered by criss-cross patterns of paper or cloth strips to prevent shattered glass from flying around and causing injury. When a stray bomb fell about fifty yards from our house in Blackeys Lane in 1941, the air pressure change from the upward eruption actually sucked out our front*

windows. The shattered panes lay on the garden, still rectangular in shape and held together by the webbing of pasted cloth strips.

Experience taught that paper strips were no use, and the ARP handbook recommended sticky cloth tape or cheesecloth. Window glass could also be protected with shatter-resistant varnish. A. M. D. Grenfell obtained quotations from several firms for such varnish, described by one firm as glass solution. A few people had their safe room made gas-proof by blocking all air inlets, and Arnold Whiteway remembered doing this for a householder in Heswall.

For those who had gardens, the Anderson shelter, a corrugated steel roof which covered a trench dug three feet into the ground, with eighteen inches of earth on top, was produced in huge numbers before the war started, one manufacturer being John Summers at Shotton. But Neston, being an unspecified area, seems to have been left out: as the council said,

The supply of Anderson steel shelters was intended to meet the needs of all people eligible for free shelters, that is to say whose income did not exceed £250 per annum. The acute shortage of steel has prevented the execution of this proposal.

It was possible to buy one at Lewis's in Liverpool, which is where the council directed enquirers. The Langleys of Willow Brow Farm, Raby, received an Anderson shelter from a different council, and the family slept in it every night during the winter of 1940–1, as "that was less bother than getting up every time the siren went".

Many people constructed their own shelters:

Our Mark 1 DIY 1939 air raid shelter at Ivy Farm, Little Neston, was a hole about eight by six feet and some five feet deep. Floored with sections of wooden packing cases, sides lined with buckled corrugated iron sheets, its roof was old railway sleepers heaped with excavated soil. The doorless entrance was a narrow stairway with steps of rough stones. It was anything but waterproof and drainage was a problem. Anyone using it for real would have been in more danger from pneumonia than from the enemy, but fortunately nobody needed to.

No wonder people preferred to take shelter under the stairs. At first, people were discouraged from leaving their homes when the alert sounded, but many preferred the company and mutual support which they found in the public shelters. However, the appeal of visiting these shelters may have waned if the closely kept secret leaked out that on 28–9 November 1940, a basement shelter in Durning Road, Liverpool, was hit and 164 people were killed, with 96 injured. A month later 72 people were killed in a shelter at Anfield.

A simple form of defence against blast was the sandbag, which appeared everywhere, especially in front of doorways. They were also recommended for smothering incendiary bombs. Empty sacks were delivered to householders in Neston in February 1941, and loads of sand were dumped in various places for people to help themselves. The piles of sand naturally attracted children, and the local head teachers were asked to tell their charges not to play in the sand.

Sandbags were a cheap means of protection against bomb blast and flying debris. Here the local Red Cross detachment passes Neston town hall.

In December 1941 the council finally heard that this area was about to be supplied with indoor Morrison table shelters at £7 each, but free to those eligible on income grounds. Applications were invited in the *Liverpool Echo*. In the next five months, 850 Morrison shelters were delivered to Neston, but only about half this number were issued, and only 40 householders actually paid for one. The Morrison shelters were rectangular steel frames, six feet five inches long, nearly four feet wide and two feet high, with a steel plate top and removable mesh sides. They could be used as tables but were not popular as the bottom rail was in the way of chairs and feet. However, *"covered with a table cloth they did not look out of place and some house-proud ladies polished them until they shone like mirrors."*

As these shelters were, by 1943, of no use in Neston, large numbers were sent to other towns. Neston householders were quite ready to get rid of theirs, 258 being reported as ready for collection, some lying dismantled in gardens. The council had only the refuse lorry to collect such things and held out for financial support from the Civil Defence, but they were not taken away until 1950. Despite the need for steel, 21 tons of it encumbered the council's yard for another three years until authorization was given to sell the steel for salvage.

The public shelters in cellars were closed in 1943 when they were no longer necessary.

The first line of Civil Defence, so far as the public were concerned, were the ARP wardens. An official description of the duties of wardens had been issued in March 1937: *"The keynote of his conduct should be courage and presence of mind."* They were to assemble at their posts and then patrol. They should know the houses in their sector, and indeed should know where each person slept, so that rescue could be directed to them. They reported incidents to their control and kept the public informed. They checked blackout and gas masks. They also investigated reports of unexploded bombs. They were *"the eyes and ears of Civil Defence"*. Harry Sowden enrolled as a warden:

> *This meant attending lectures on air raid precautions against bombs and gases, first aid and so on. I enjoyed these classes because I wanted to be able to help if we were needed. I remember one incident when I was a warden. A bomb dropped in Parkgate Road opposite the house of Dr Yeoman* [Elmhurst]. *It did not go off. My co-warden and I were the first to it. This other chap started to pull at the fin on the top of the bomb, saying that he wanted it as a souvenir. I had to restrain him.*

In Cheshire, the Chief Constable, Jack Beck, was in charge of appointing ARP wardens, and he issued each one with a signed certificate. The chief warden, in charge of the whole Neston UDC district, was J. E. B. Plummer, who lived in Burton, and his deputy was M. B. Richardson. Under them were A. R. Cannel, the head warden of the six Neston sectors, and Louis Matthews, the chief fire guard. The ARP headquarters was at the old Westminster Bank at the Cross (where Rigby's the barber

Air Raids

> Extracts from instruction leaflet supplied to Neston householders with the Morrison table shelter.

The steel shelter was delivered in pieces and according to the Ministry could be assembled by two people in two hours. It could accommodate two adults and one or two children.

It was to be positioned on the ground floor or the basement, preferably in a room facing a garden so that a bomb might bury itself in the soil before exploding. Windows of the room had to be protected to prevent glass splinters.

FIGURE 6

With the mesh sides removed the shelter could be used as a table or bed.

FIGURE 8

The Morrison shelter was a prominent feature in homes all over the country, though apparently not received with much enthusiasm in the Neston area.

Chapter Four

is now), although at the start of the war the headquarters was in the Neston Hotel, opposite the town hall. The town was divided into six sectors, each with its post commanded by a sector warden. During a raid there were supposed to be three wardens to a post, one staying there while the others patrolled to clear the streets. Within each sector there were areas, each with a group warden and a number of fire-watchers.

The warden system was put in place before war was declared, but the six months of inactivity that followed, the 'phoney war', were an anti-climax. To combat this, Sir Warren Fisher, North-West Regional Commissioner, sent this message in March 1940: *"Just because nothing to speak of has yet happened, do not think you have been wasting your time. When it suits them the Germans will start up."*

Jim Jones was a warden:

> *He was a member of the ARP, who wore navy blue battledress. His duties were to go round in the evenings when it was dark to make sure that there was no light showing through any windows. When the siren sounded he had to go out ringing a handbell and assisting those who needed it. When the all-clear sounded he had to go round blowing a whistle.*

"The wardens", said the ARP handbook, *"should at once call the attention of the occupier to any unobscured light in a building."* Mrs Crossley remembered her warden shouting, *"Put that light out!"* after somebody in her house had been to the bathroom. Wardens were also equipped with wooden rattles of the type seen since only at football matches. These were to give warning of poison gas, and were thankfully never used.

The wardens were responsible for the shelters. There were supposed to be shelter marshals, and the Chief Constable advised the council that they should be *"people of good local standing, well known and possessing tact, courage and initiative, to help defeat that all-important enemy weapon, nerve strain"*. But in practice this duty devolved upon the wardens, and on 10 July 1940 the chief warden, J. E. B. Plummer, wrote to his colleagues to remind them of their duties:

> *Open up the shelters and place yourself in charge of those who come to use them, and insist upon discipline and cleanliness. Ascertain after a raid whether the sanitary convenience has been used or the shelter fouled.*

They had to send a report to the surveyor at the town hall if it was necessary to send a cleansing squad. It is known that the shelter at Parkgate infants' school had two custodians and a keyholder, Mornington Swift.

Sector 1 had its post next to the Coach and Horses in Bridge Street. The sector warden was Tom Smith, and his three areas were

> High Street below the Cross (H. Robinson)
> Pear Tree Crescent (H. Sowden)
> Fleming's Cottages (J. D. Williams)

Sector 2 had its post at the station booking office off Raby Road. The sector warden was W. H. Evans, with four areas:

> Gladstone Road (G. Watson)
> Raby Road and Gardens (M. E. Webster)
> Blackeys Lane (J. R. Jones)
> Tannery Lane (E. S. Redfern)

Sector 3 had its post behind the Institute. The sector warden was E. Roxburgh, and his three areas were

> Olive Drive (Mrs Bromilow)
> Olive Road (G. Mannion)
> Hinderton Road (H. G. Boston)

Sector 4 had its post in a house in Hinderton Lane. The sector warden was G. R. Griffin, and he had two areas:

> the top of Hinderton Road (J. D. Russell)
> lower Hinderton Road (Mrs Larden Williams)

Sector 5 had its post in Birch's shelter in Liverpool Road opposite the Methodist church. The sector warden was J. R. Corkhill, with two areas:

> Liverpool Road (G. B. Foyle)
> Park Street, Raby Road, High Street (J. Cottrell)

Sector 6 had its post at 'Steel Post', which was beside the library. The sector warden was C. Coventry, who had four areas:

> Church Lane (P. J. Macaulay)
> top of Parkgate Road (C. Coventry)
> middle of Parkgate Road (Louis Matthews)
> Mill Street (V. C. Hickey)

Neston's six ARP sectors. There were also twenty wardens who were not allocated to particular areas.

Chapter Four

The wardens took their duties very seriously. At their monthly meeting in November 1941 they asked the head warden, A. R. Cannel, to write to the Town Clerk asking for more and better shelter accommodation. It was pointed out that to enter the shelter below the ARP headquarters at the Cross, it was necessary to open a trapdoor in the pavement and bend almost double. For the safety of pedestrians the trapdoor had to be shut, so people inside felt trapped and were reluctant to use the shelter. The shelter under Williams's at the Cross suffered from the same problem, and that under Birch's was awkward and very unpopular.

The air raids on Merseyside began, as described above, once the *Luftwaffe* obtained airfields in northern France in June 1940. The first siren warning after this was on 25 June, when German planes flew overhead but dropped nothing. The first bombs dropped on Cheshire fell on the night of 29 July, when several high-explosive bombs fell harmlessly in fields, including some at Neston. Mrs Crook remembered the craters in Wood Lane (two or three, according to Colin Foote) which people came out from Birkenhead by bus to see. It was reported that no damage was done, although shrapnel hit some cows. This was before the first casualty on Merseyside (in Prenton on 9 August), and before the bombing of London began. The first heavy raids on Merseyside were on the last four nights of August, when up to 176 bombers at a time dropped a total of 455 tons of high explosive and 1,029 incendiaries. Dreadful though this was, it was nowhere near the prediction of Sir Warren Fisher, already quoted, that the Germans *"could drop 1,000 tons of bombs every 24 hours and go on doing it"*. Three high-explosive bombs and a large incendiary landed in Raby on the night of 28 August. One bomb did not explode until the following evening, and the local constable was posted to stop people peering down the hole.

There followed relatively light raids, on average every other night, for three months. Bad weather kept the raiders away in December until the 'Christmas bombing' at the end of the month, when there was severe damage in Liverpool and its surroundings. For the people of Neston, these six months had meant constant alarm and disturbed nights, but nothing worse. The schools tended to open late if there had been warnings during the night, and the Ness Holt school log book shows that the registers were marked at 10 a.m.

January and February 1941 were free from raids because of bad weather. On the night of 12 March there was a very severe raid which did involve Neston, when two German planes were damaged over the Dee and their

Air Raids

crews baled out. Then came the 'May blitz', when Liverpool and its surroundings suffered immense damage over seven successive nights. There were relatively light raids on 1 and 2 May, while on the night of 3 May 298 bombers set Liverpool ablaze with 49,700 incendiaries and 363 tons of high-explosive bombs. There were further raids on the next four nights, on the last of which a third German aircrew baled out over the Dee. These raids would typically start at about 11 p.m. and might continue for four hours.

Some bombs fell in the Neston area during March, April and May 1941. Some of these may have been unloaded by planes trying to avoid pursuit, while others may have been aimed at the decoy targets on the golf course near Parkgate and on the marsh at Burton. The unexploded bomb that Harry Sowden investigated in Parkgate Road broke a water main. The nearby houses were evacuated, the road was cordoned off and the library was closed. The congregation of the Presbyterian church went to a service in the Methodist church instead. The bomb landed outside Elm Grove House, next to Dr Yeoman's house. The doctor was away at the time, and on his return said to Andrew Prince, *"People will think I must have known about it and left the district."* A second bomb fell at the same time in the grounds of Leighton Court, blowing down the wall beside Buggen Lane.

Another bomb fell half-way between Blackeys Lane and Olive Drive, some fifty yards opposite the Footes' house, Dawn Cottage. Harry Foote was out in Wallasey on fire service duty at the time, but Colin Foote remembers:

> *Mum, my younger brother and I were asleep in the lounge. The crackle of ack-ack [anti-aircraft] guns we were well used to and slept through. But there was a deafening explosion, the old house shook on its foundations and we were engulfed in a cloud of soot from the chimney. 'Old Jerry has made a better job of sweeping the chimney than ever Joe Blackie did!' exclaimed Mum. When Dad arrived home, shattered and weary, in the early hours of the morning, we were still trying to clear up the mess.*

They found a piece of bomb shrapnel twenty inches long embedded deeply in a pear tree in the garden.

A stick of bombs fell across Little Neston. Hugh Norman recalled,

> *The bombs fell about midnight. The first was on waste ground in Bull Hill in the garden of Glenton House. The second was at the top end of Newtown on Mr Idden's smallholding, where Ashtree Close is now. The crater was five to six yards across. Stones and earth landed on the roofs of houses in Mellock*

Lane. The third landed in the field in Mellock Lane where the present St Winefride's School is. The fourth just missed the railway line which is now the Wirral Way, landing on the far side of the cutting. The fifth one landed in a field near the houses in Hinderton Road.

Mrs Jones, who lived in Victoria Road, vividly remembers that night:

There was a shelter at the top of Badger Bait but I was fed up of getting the children up to go to it, so we got under the stairs. The bomb shook the place and we came out and stood by the fireplace. Soot came down the chimney and covered us.

There was one night when Eddie Scott borrowed his father's shotgun, without permission, and went looking for rabbits at the top of Woodfall Lane. Finding himself on unfamiliar ground, he had a strange feeling of *déjà vu*: he was reminded of a recurring dream he had had of being shot at by Japanese.

I was trying to laugh this off when I became aware of a horrible noise as of rushing water. I instinctively dived into the ditch, as a bomb fell not fifteen yards from where I lay. I never dared tell my parents how I got so muddy, as it would have involved admitting having borrowed the gun, but I never had the dream again.

Hugh Whittemore kept a diary of events at Goldstraw Farm in Ness. He recorded on 7 April 1941 that there had been a blitz that night and some bombs dropped but did not explode. The next day he filled in two craters, but at 4 p.m. one of the bombs exploded, making another crater, fifteen feet deep and twelve yards in diameter. Hugh spent all day trying to keep children away from the unexploded bombs, and the following day fifteen soldiers from Burton came to help fill in the crater. Then on 6 May he wrote, "Blitz at night. Two bombs in Young's oats resulting in the greenhouse being knocked about. Time bomb in oats and peas."

When a bomb fell on the marsh near the Harp Inn, the crater filled with water and small boys went swimming in it.

These bombs were probably attracted by the lights on the decoy target on Burton marsh, and other lights could attract unwanted attention. Don Hulse's family farm in Dunstan Lane had chicken houses with glass roofs that reflected the moonlight. "One night we had 36 incendiary bombs and my father put them out with hen muck." Mr Scott kept sheep, and "he went out last thing at night to see if they were all right. The lights of his car were seen and incendiary bombs were dropped around him."

It was probably the other decoy target, on the Heswall golf course, that attracted a flurry of incendiaries during the May blitz. The war diary of the Royal Northumberland Fusiliers, whose Z Company was at Leighton School in Parkgate, recorded that on the night of 1 May, *"during the raids on Merseyside several bombs fell near Z Company."* On the following night, *"Z Company again had bombs falling near them."* And on the night of 5 May, *"Z Company had an exciting night, a great number of incendiary bombs being dropped near their Mess* [at Woodcote, in Wood Lane] *— they were quickly extinguished by the Company's fire picquet."* It was probably on this last occasion that the only substantial damage by bombs in Neston was caused. Some incendiaries set fire to the north end of the Parkgate swimming baths buildings and to a boathouse belonging to Mostyn House just beyond. The curate of Neston, J. Russell Edwards, was due to be married on 7 May to Joyce Nicholls. They had arranged their reception at the Boat House Café and were alarmed by a report that *"the boathouse had burned down"*. But it was not the café!

> *When the incendiary bombs hit the back of Parkgate Baths, we were down there straight away the next morning, even though it was Sunday and we were in our best clothes, collecting bits of smouldering wood to bring home for firewood. Didn't we get into trouble for mucking up our Sunday clothes!*

The Mostyn House boathouse was destroyed with its contents, which included sailing boats and tackle, oars, two canoes, three sand yachts and an outboard motor, for which a claim was sent to the War Damage Commission.

Even before the May blitz, Hitler had begun ordering the *Luftwaffe* to go East in preparation for his invasion of Russia, which started on 22 June. The destruction of Liverpool, vital to Germany if Britain was to be brought to her knees by economic blockade, was abandoned. But spasmodic light raids continued, and one of these caused the only casualties in the Neston district. On 1 November 1941 George Langley of Willow Brow Farm, Raby, which had an anti-aircraft battery in nearby fields, wrote in his diary, *"Very bad blitz at night. Two bombs dropped in the middle field and killed eleven of our milking cows."*

SOURCES

This chapter was written by Geoffrey Place, largely from the research of Susan Chambers.

Valuable information was obtained from Bryan Perrett, *Liverpool, a City at War* (1990); N. C. H. Tomlinson, *Walking through the Blitz* (1996); anon., *Air Raids in Cheshire*; Air Raid Precautions Handbook No.8, The duties of air raid wardens (HMSO 1938); and the War Diary of the 9th Battalion, Royal Northumberland Fusiliers (Public Record Office).

We are grateful for the help of Keith Bolton, Roy Booth, Geoffrey Boston, Reg Bushell, Jim Cochrane, Marie Crook, Lettice Crossley, Flo Dodd, Colin Foote, Julian Grenfell, Don Hulse, Mrs Jones, Thelma Kameen (née Hale), George Langley, Graham Langley, Jane Macdonald, Hugh Norman, Andrew Prince, Eddie Scott, Harry Sowden, Geoffrey Thomas, Arnold Whiteway, Hugh Whittemore and Ruth Nicholls.

CHAPTER FIVE

ON DUTY: THE EMERGENCY AND VOLUNTARY SERVICES

Civil Defence was a term which covered a host of organizations and precautions which supported the civilian population in time of war. Overall supervision was provided by the Ministry of Home Security, and successive ministers, Sir John Anderson and Herbert Morrison, gave their names to types of shelter. The country was split into twelve regions to allow dispersal of Government from London, and the Regional Commissioner for the North-West, Sir Warren Fisher, co-ordinated Civil Defence in his area. If there had been an invasion, he would have taken over as civil governor. Under him, the local Civil Defence services were the responsibility of the local authority, personified in Neston by the Town Clerk, Frank Poole. The services, as described by the ARP handbook, were

> first of all the Wardens, who are the essential link between the public and the Civil Defence services, and who are responsible for advising and helping their neighbours on all Civil Defence matters, for reporting incidents and for summoning the appropriate help. Then there are the messengers, clerks and telephonists who staff the Report Centres from which the dispatch of the various services are organized; there are the Rescue and Demolition parties and Decontamination squads; the First Aid parties and ambulance drivers and attendants; and the doctors, nurses and first aiders who man the First Aid posts. Finally there is the vast organization for wartime defence against fire: the Auxiliary Fire Service and the Fire Guard.

To this list we can add the Women's Voluntary Service for Civil Defence and their rural allies, the Women's Institutes. Some of these were paid, most were voluntary, but all were prepared to work without regard to hours, reward or personal safety when the crunch came.

The most immediate and obvious of the air raid precautions was the blackout. Not a chink of light was allowed to be emitted from any dwelling house or business premises from half an hour after sunset to half an hour before dawn, and the times were published each day in

Chapter Five

> # Women's Voluntary Services for Civil Defence.
>
> Enrolling Centre: NESTON TOWN HALL.
> Hours: 10-30—12, 2-30—4, Mondays and Fridays.
> 6-30—8, Wednesdays.
>
> It is essential that all women should be enrolled for National Service, trained or untrained, and also those who can only spare an hour a day.
>
> We have been asked by the Home Office to index all volunteers. Will you, therefore, help us by calling to tell us what war work you have undertaken ? If you have not yet enrolled, we will help you to decide which of the 36 jobs you can do best.

The many duties carried out by the Women's Voluntary Service, 36 according to this recruitment notice, meant that the authorities were always seeking more volunteers.

newspapers such as the *Liverpool Daily Post*. The gas street lamps were removed from Neston in November 1939, and white lines were painted on the roads and obstructions such as lamp posts. People on foot were allowed to carry torches, but only if the light was muffled with white paper. Accidents were numerous, and in November 1941 Mr Cannel, Neston's head warden, wrote to the council to say, *"It has been brought to our notice that several people have collided with lamp posts in the blackout. A fresh marking of white paint would prove beneficial."* Roy Booth's mother dyed her curtains black, saying, *"By the time this war is over I'll be able to buy new ones."* At Mostyn House Daryl Grenfell wrote, *"After floundering about amidst yards of curtain rods and material, brown paper and black and blue paint, we have tackled the lighting situation."* Being a man who believed that curtains harbour germs, he also made much use of blinds and wooden shutters. But there was no way he could black out the school chapel, so evening services were abandoned. The school's carillon of bells, a memorial to those pupils killed in the First World War, was silenced, as all church bells were, because they would be used to warn the population if the Germans invaded Britain.

NATIONAL SERVICE CAMPAIGN.

Volunteers are Required for Various Services.

NESTON & DISTRICT still require Personnel for the following:—

AUXILIARY FIRE SERVICE	Men
RECEPTION OF EVACUEES (Children and others):	
CARS & CAR DRIVERS	Men & Women
NURSING & OTHER SERVICE	Women
WOMEN'S VOLUNTARY SERVICES	Women
FIRST AID & CASUALTY SERVICE	Men & Women
AMBULANCE & CAR DRIVERS	Women
MESSENGERS	Boys
BRITISH RED CROSS SOCIETY	Women
ST. JOHN'S AMBULANCE BRIGADE	Men & Women

Keep Right—Be Prepared. Defence is the responsibility of every Citizen, and even if you are in a Reserved Occupation you can play your part by enrolling for Part Time in the above Services.

Efficiency can only be obtained by sacrifices, and training after enrolment, of two or three hours a week, will be found to be enjoyable and intensely interesting. At the end of this you are no longer in the ranks of the "What have they done?" but a Member of an Organisation who can and will act systematically, efficiently and calmly, having that sense of security so much desired, should the need arise.

Service is a duty to yourself, your family, and last but not least, your Country, if the privileges now enjoyed are to be maintained and reinforced.

This can be made secure by your enrolling at once.

How to do this:—

Complete the Enrolment Form, copies of which will be found in your National Service Hand Book, and send it to the Council Offices, Town Hall, Neston.

Further copies of the Hand Book and Enrolment Form, together with information or assistance desired, will gladly be given on application to the above address, where a Woman's Voluntary Service Recruiting Office is open, or at the local Branch Office of the Ministry of Labour.

IMPORTANT.

The Film "**The Warning**" (which every man and woman should see) is being shown at The Cinema, Neston, on Monday, Tuesday and Wednesday evenings of this week.

Other volunteer organizations called on Neston's townspeople, too. As this notice said, "Service is a duty to yourself, your family, and last but not least, your Country..."

Chapter Five

Car headlights had to be dimmed, as local lads recalled:

Vehicles, and bicycles even, could only be used at night with masked lights, so that in theory nothing could be seen from overhead. Only a partial beam was directed onto the road immediately in front. Owners had to buy light shields: these were rounded tin cylinders, open at one end to fit over the headlamp, and the other end had three one-inch slits, and lids like eyelids over the slits so that the light shone down.

The police issued a notice explaining these regulations. Lamp reflectors had to be painted with black paint, sidelights had to be masked with paper, direction indicators had to be masked to allow an arrow-shaped light no more than one-eighth of an inch wide. The newly erected traffic lights at Hinderton cross-roads were fitted with hoods to direct the light downward, and the lamp was taken from the Bushell fountain.

Each household was issued with an Air Raid Precautions card which advised the names of its senior warden and local warden, and the location of the nearest ARP warden's post and first aid post: *"These two posts will always be manned during air raids."* The card explained the care of gas masks, the lighting restrictions, the warning signals and self-help in case of fire: *"Provide two buckets filled with water and, if possible, a stirrup hand pump with two-purpose nozzle, either producing spray for dealing with the bomb itself, or producing a jet for tackling the resulting fire."*

The 'stirrup' was a metal foot which you stood on to keep the pump upright while pumping water from the bucket with one hand and directing the nozzle with the other, although it was recommended that two people should operate it. You were warned against throwing water onto an incendiary bomb, as this would cause it to spit molten metal: you were recommended to cover the bomb with sand and carry it outside in a bucket. A notice in the *Birkenhead News* of 22 May 1940 said, *"Neighbours are asked to club together to buy pumps and to learn how to use them. Has your street got one?"* They could be bought through the Fire Service for £1 each.

Neston had a fire brigade before the war, manned by part-timers and housed underneath the town hall. They had a pump which had to be towed by private cars. When the war started, an Auxiliary Fire Service was established and seventeen firemen were employed full time. A fire station was set up at the Cross, in a building that had been Hancock's butcher's shop, and was later Evans's pharmacy, with Neston Social Club also on the premises. It is now a jeweller's. The front was opened up to take two Sigmund light trailer pumps which were towed by vans. There was a kitchen at the back and bedrooms above. John Robinson was a fireman at the time and said there were five men to a pump crew and seven to a watch. The man in charge was Fred Tilston, who had earlier managed Neston's New Cinema, supervised at first by the station officer at Heswall.

> I can remember Fred Tilston standing outside, resplendent in silver-buttoned fire chief's uniform, spotless white shirt and tie. A charismatic character, Fred, rotund, powerfully stocky, horn-rimmed glasses surmounting a bulbous nose, well read and with a fund of stories.

Before the war the Neston firemen wore overalls, but when they moved to the new fire station they were issued with proper uniforms and Neston badges.

In January 1942 Sir Percy Bates of Hinderton Hall, whose son was a fireman, entertained the AFS, saying that they must have been bored by the inactivity of recent months, but *"they also serve who only stand and wait"*. After supper Lady Bates played the violin, and there were songs.

Eddie Wright served in Neston's Auxiliary Fire Service.

In the Neston area itself there were few fires to attend, and John Robinson said that in the summer, nine out of ten calls were to gorse fires in Heswall. The firemen were always afraid that the tanks of the oil reclamation business in Cross Street would catch fire, but they never did. The Neston brigade was called out to help in other areas, notably to Barrowmore Hospital in Delamere Forest, which was bombed, with many killed. They supported the Birkenhead Fire Service, and John Robinson remembers going to Wallasey when a flour mill was practically destroyed. In December 1940 they were called to Huskisson Dock in Liverpool and to Hoylake. The firemen also gave training in dealing with incendiaries, for example to the fire-watchers at William Fleming's builder's premises, and they bought practice bombs from Brock's Fireworks, for demonstration.

Chapter Five

The fire station was manned 24 hours a day, and part-timers like Harry Foote were employed as well as the full-time crews. In August 1941 the Auxiliary Fire Service became the National Fire Service, formed to standardize equipment and practice throughout the country. Neston was classed as Division K, Area 26 under the Liverpool headquarters.

One of the worries for all fire services was their water supply, and in both London and Liverpool there were times when the mains were breached, water had to be pumped from the rivers, and some buildings had to be left to burn for lack of water. Throughout the country large tanks appeared marked 'EWS' (Emergency Water Supply). The only one remembered locally was in Willaston, at the school. For Neston, the chief fire officer from Birkenhead recommended numerous hydrant points and 10,000-gallon dams at each end of the shore. Instead it was decided to link with the Alwen main supply, or to fall back on the indoor pool at Mostyn House (the fire engine would sometimes come and spray everything for practice), the old storm water sewer on the Parkgate Parade, or the outdoor swimming baths.

In Parkgate there was a fire post, originally at Leeman's garage on the Parade, manned by volunteers from Mostyn Gardens with stirrup pumps. In June 1941 Daryl Grenfell offered the Town Clerk the free use of part of the school's garage and an adjacent room as a fire post, with a view to moving it from Leeman's, but it is thought the offer was not taken up.

Before Bob Chrimes enlisted in the RAF, he joined the National Fire Service in Neston.

Fire-watching teams were organized to look for falling incendiary bombs and deal with them. In December 1940 fire-watching duty was made compulsory, and armbands marked 'SFP' (Supplementary Fire Party) were issued. The name was soon (in May 1941) changed to Fire Guards, and they became part of the warden service. In Neston, Arnold Whiteway, who worked for Fleming's, helped to make a wooden shed which was hauled in sections to the top of the church tower with ropes on a jenny wheel. It housed a couple of fire-watchers, but he said it was not very pleasant up there in a raid: there was nowhere to run. There were supposed to be five in a fire guard team (three watching and two sleeping), with two stirrup pumps. In December 1941 the curate, J. Russell Edwards, wrote,

> *The fire-watching squads have begun duty and the Lads* [of the Church Lads' Club] *have responded very well and we have to report for duty only every three weeks. There were camp beds and a Lilo to sleep on in the church hall and some inadequate blankets. Suddenly, there was a tremendous thumping going on. I thought that we had slept through the siren, but no, it was only the caretaker shifting the chairs around in the hall, ready for the Red Cross working party; our watches still said 4.45 a.m.*

Mrs Crook had fire-watchers in her house in Parkgate because, being a post office, there was a telephone. They came in relays and sat all night in her kitchen making cups of tea. They did not take it very seriously until a bomb came.

The council organized a heavy rescue squad, based at the council depot behind the town hall, with Bill Ashbrook, the general foreman, in charge. All the council manual workers were in the squad, with some former miners. Ashbrook was the only one with the building experience which was important for rescue work. He once ordered Brudder Jones to check a roof space. Brudder hesitated to climb up to it as he thought it unsafe. *"I will say if it is safe or no"*, said Ashbrook firmly. The only vehicle they had was the council refuse lorry. If the worst happened, there were mortuaries established in various places: at Albert Woodward's next to the parish church hall (Woodward was an undertaker), at Hilbre House on Parkgate Parade, and in Little Neston behind the Royal Oak, including the bowling green pavilion.

Jack Beck, the Chief Constable, organized a team of local businessmen who had cars to attend at the police station and act as couriers in an emergency. The new police station in Hinderton Road had only just been opened. One man had a big American car, and a piece of shrapnel dropped on it while it was parked in the police station yard.

Chapter Five

> *When the alarm sounded we congregated at the police station: fire, ambulance, rescue and mobile couriers. Sometimes we were called out on consecutive nights: it was very tiring but there was no one to take your place. We sat around waiting for the all-clear and we would acquire tins of soup and beans, cook it all in a pan and distribute it among the people on duty. It was the humour which kept you sane.*

Meanwhile, the old police station in Park Street, behind the Methodist church, was used as a decontamination depot (in case of poison gas), a casualty station manned by the Red Cross, the rescue and road repair unit and the public assistance office. There were plans to extend the town hall to make an emergency depot, but the cost was too high.

There were two Red Cross detachments. The first, officially known as 'British Red Cross, Voluntary Aid Detachment Cheshire 6', was commanded by Pamela Jackson, who lived at Leighton Court. She had served in the same detachment in the First World War, when it had run a hospital at the Institute. The women provided the first aid and casualty staff at the old police station, and ambulance drivers, much to the chagrin of certain members of the men's Red Cross detachment. The nurse in charge of the first aid unit was Doris Vickers, who had been a sister at Neston Cottage Hospital. One of the members was Kathleen Kinnaston:

> *We used to go on duty at the old police station in Park Street, in my case one night a week, and also helped out at the Cottage Hospital one Sunday a month. I was always on with my friend Joan Chrimes. We used to sleep in the court room and when there was a call-out we went out through the back door, which entailed going along the passage between the cells, a bit creepy in the dark. Our main duties were taking heavily expectant mothers to Clatterbridge from the two maternity hostels. They had been evacuated here from Merseyside while the blitz was on.*

The other Red Cross detachment, Cheshire 25, was for men, and was run by James Hacking, woodwork teacher at the Neston council school in Burton Road, who had earlier been chairman of Neston Council. He too had been in the Red Cross in the First World War. His pupils knew him as 'Joey Stump', because he had lost part of a finger to a circular saw. The men's depot was above Martin's Bank. A Red Cross hospital supply depot at the parish church hall made such things as bandages and surgical dressings. Both men's and women's detachments were manned day and night throughout the war.

In February 1944 Miss Jackson offered the services of her women's section to prepare a meal for the men, on such occasions as they were required to attend for duty, provided that the men were willing to co-operate in its preparation.

The maternity hostels were at Ashburton in Manorial Road, Parkgate, and The Garth in Hinderton Road. Ashburton belonged to A. M. D. Grenfell, whose tenant moved out just before the war, and this building was at first requisitioned for use by the Army in June 1940. When the Army released it the following January it was the very next day requisitioned by the Town Clerk of Neston UDC under the Government evacuation scheme on behalf of the Ministry of Health. The other house, The Garth, had been the home of G. S. Boston before he moved to Willaston, and he gave the house to the Ministry of Health for the duration of the war. One mother who stayed at The Garth, and whose baby son was born there, hit the headlines in November 1945. As the *Birkenhead News* reported,

> *A Birkenhead G.I. bride took the law into her own hands, and with her eight-month-old son and a small suitcase containing condensed milk and a few nappies, stowed away aboard the steamer* Victory.
>
> *25-year-old Mrs Winifred Maresco decided on this course of action when her endeavours to rejoin her G.I. husband Ralph by more orthodox methods failed. On November 15th, 1945 Mrs Maresco went to Bidston dock with her baby son Joseph. With the help of a British soldier she hid herself and the baby in the emergency generator room. Two days out at sea the ship developed engine trouble and a member of the crew discovered the stowaways.*

GIs (for 'General Issue') were American servicemen, and those who married in England, as Ralph and Winifred did in 1943, had difficulty in getting their wives to America when they were demobilized, for reasons of both cost and shipping space. The Maresco family were reunited in the USA, and Joseph grew up to become dean of a Pennsylvania university and to revisit his birthplace in Neston.

Andrew Prince was the Council's public health officer, and the casualty and ambulance services fell under his supervision. There were three ambulances available in Neston. One, provided by Cheshire County Council, was an Austin. Another was a converted Buick, the gift of G. S. Boston. The third was a Humber given to the Red Cross by Olive Higgin of Puddington Hall from a trust fund set up by her father, A. B. Earle. It was said that this ambulance, which was kept in the old barn by the Brewer's Arms, could only be driven in first gear. The other two ambulances were kept behind the town hall and in Richard Morgan's garage at the Cross. The ARP wardens looked after them.

Chapter Five

The emergency services in Neston had three ambulances to call on: *top*, the Austin which Cheshire County Council provided; *bottom*, the splendid-looking Humber given by Mrs Higgin.

The cottage hospital in Little Neston, opened in 1920 as a memorial to those local men killed in the First World War, continued during the Second World War much as it had done before. Olwen Whiteway says

> *When war was declared in 1939, some of the local doctors were called up, but operations continued. Even more so, because then we were having evacuee patients from Birkenhead and Wallasey, with surgeons coming to operate from those areas. We were certainly kept quite busy, and felt that 'the cottage' was contributing to the war effort.*

The reception of patients from Merseyside was very timely, for in 1941 the hospital's finances gave cause for serious concern, with closure being a rumoured possibility. Each year a firework display had been held at Parkgate in front of Mostyn House, raising about £100 for the hospital, and the loss of this source of money to the blackout was a contributing factor. Therefore the income received for the treatment of evacuated patients helped save the day.

"These patients would normally have gone to the city hospitals, but now the comparative safety and peace of a small country hospital was eagerly sought." As a result, 1942 was the busiest year in the hospital's history until then, with 354 in-patients admitted (to 25 beds and two cots) and 615 out-patients treated.

One of the Neston doctors, and the hospital's senior doctor at the time, was Dr George Gunn. His son, Ward Gunn, was awarded an MC and a posthumous VC in North Africa in 1941, and an appeal was launched in 1943 for £500 to endow a hospital bed in his memory. *"The response to the appeal was startling, for in a brief period the sum of £1,562 was contributed, more than three times the amount required, and it represented the whole district, even small children calling at the treasurer's house to give their pennies."* A plaque was placed above a bed in the men's ward, which read:

IN MEMORY OF THE LATE
2ND LIEUT. G. WARD GUNN V.C. M.C.
OF J BATTERY 3RD R.H.A.
THIS BED IS ENDOWED
BY HIS MANY FRIENDS AND ADMIRERS
TO COMMEMORATE HIS
GALLANT DEEDS IN LIBYA 1941

The major hospital locally was Clatterbridge County General Hospital, with 313 beds. On the same site but separately administered was the Fever Hospital for infectious diseases. As well as these there was an

2nd Lieutenant G. Ward Gunn, VC, MC, Royal Horse Artillery, was killed at Sidi Rezegh on 21 November 1941.

emergency hospital established by the Ministry of Health, first at Thornton Manor but then in huts on the Clatterbridge site. In 1944 these huts were handed to the American forces as part of a military hospital.

The Women's Voluntary Service for Civil Defence (WVS), founded in 1938 at the request of the Home Office, organized women to do a myriad useful tasks, such as billeting evacuees. They, or some of them, wore a green uniform with a red jersey. They were enrolled at Neston Town Hall, encouraged by a card which offered 36 possible jobs: *"It is essential that all women should be enrolled for National Service, trained or untrained, and also those who can only spare an hour a day."*

In 1941 the WVS moved from the town hall to Kelly's Buildings, on the corner of Bridge Street and Chester Road. The centre organizer at the time was Mrs F. Anstead-Browne, who organized the display of the Junkers plane at Parkgate to raise funds for the Spitfire Fund in 1940. In 1942 she was working for the Ministry of Works in Chester, arranging the removal of iron railings. The names of other WVS centre organizers were Miss Field in 1942 and Miss Montgomery.

In the villages the same kinds of work were done by the Women's Institutes, and the records of those in Willaston and Burton give a full picture of their activities. In July 1939 the WVS asked the Women's Institute members to register for some wartime service, as has been seen in Neston, and this took place in Willaston War Memorial Hut. Speakers for the monthly meetings were often sought from the Ministry of Information, and such topical subjects were heard as fire fighting, gas, incendiary bombs, the use of steel shelters in the home and problems of sleep during air raids.

Much of their work concerned food, savings or salvage, which will be discussed in another chapter. Another major preoccupation was clothing, as "make do and mend" was one of the catchphrases of the war years.

> **WOMEN'S VOLUNTARY SERVICES for CIVIL DEFENCE**
>
> Tel. Neston, 1359.
>
> Town Hall,
> Neston,
> Wirral.
>
> 8th April, 1941.
>
> Dear Mr. Prince,
>
> Re Kelly's Buildings.
>
> Some time ago I asked you if you would be good enough to examine the yard at the back of Kelly's Buildings and if you could take some action in this matter as we are shortly moving in, and the yard is in a totally insanitary condition, and I am afraid I do not know who is responsible for this but I feel that a word from you would put this right. I should be glad if you could spare a moment to do this.
>
> Yours sincerely,
>
> A. Austead Burton
>
> Centre Organiser, W.V.S.
>
> A. Prince, Esq.,
> Sanitary Inspector,
> Council Offices,
> Town Hall,
> Neston.

Sometimes council officials needed to be chivvied!

Speakers came to give tips on renovating clothes, adapting them for children, and refurbishing millinery. Courses were held on sewing, soft slipper and glove making. The Willaston members had a hospital sewing group, and rugs were made for the soldier wards at Clatterbridge. Clothing was collected for people who had been bombed out of their homes, and toys were made for children evacuated from Malta and Gibraltar. The Neston Red Cross had its own sewing group, and there were several others, including the Neston Sewing for the Forces class and

WAR ORGANISATION
OF THE
BRITISH RED CROSS SOCIETY
AND
ORDER OF ST JOHN OF JERUSALEM

Presented to

Kathleen Ellen Gray

B.R.C.S. Cheshire 62

in recognition of devoted service to
the cause of humanity
during the second world war

1939~1945

George R.I. — Sovereign Head, Order of St. John of Jerusalem.

Elizabeth R — President, British Red Cross Society.

Members of the British Red Cross Society and the Order of St John of Jerusalem received recognition for their service.

the War Comforts committee. The latter sent 4,161 woollen garments to the forces in 1940, and in 1941 they had an extremely active and successful year, making 2,415 garments, sending 247 parcels to local men in various services and to the Mersey Mission to Seamen, and giving 40 balaclavas and scarves to Neston Fire Brigade. Mrs Catherine Scott used to knit long white medical socks for the wounded with wool supplied by Mrs Gunn, the doctor's wife. A weekly knitting party at Puddington Hall in 1940 produced 850 garments and some 500 WVS armbands. By 1943 they had knitted 1,001 pairs of socks, 100 of them by one member.

When Hitler invaded Russia in 1941 the Soviet Union became, for four brief years, our ally and friend. The Red Cross appealed for dried rabbit skins to line clothing for Russia. The Burton WI collected and cured skins, while in Willaston they lined six pairs of mittens and one coat for children and made two fur coats. In 1943 the Burton & Puddington WI was making camouflage netting, and at the end of the war, the Cheshire Federation adopted Twickenham as part of a scheme to collect gifts for rehabilitated houses.

Despite rationing, the women's organizations also did their best to entertain their enforced visitors. Several Christmas parties were arranged for evacuee children at Neston Town Hall, the Burton WI entertained soldiers from the local searchlight battery and from Burton Manor, and at Willaston they organized a Christmas party for local Land Girls.

SOURCES

This chapter was written by Geoffrey Place.

Useful publications included *Air Raids: what you must know, what you must do* (HMSO 1941); Neston and District War Memorial Cottage Hospital's Annual Reports for 1942 and 1947–8; and *A Short History of Clatterbridge Hospital*, 1966.

The ARP card and the quotations from A. M. D. Grenfell are in the archives of Mostyn House.

Hilary Morris analysed the records of the Willaston and Burton & Puddington Women's Institutes.

We are grateful for the memories of Roy Booth, Marie Crook, Colin Foote, Kathleen Kinnaston, Jane Macdonald, Andrew Prince, John Robinson, and Arnold and Olwen Whiteway.

CHAPTER SIX

THE DEFENCES

The British military authorities did not seriously think that the German army would invade Britain by way of the Dee estuary, or its surroundings, but of course they did not say so, and the civilian population was allowed to suppose that the enemy might appear anywhere. General Ironside was responsible for Home Defence at the start of the war, and he encouraged road blocks throughout the country. Concrete obstructions were placed on many roads: for example, cubes of concrete three feet high, with iron rods sticking out of the top, were placed beneath the railway bridge on the road from Neston to Parkgate, so that traffic had to weave a path between them. However, Ironside retired in June 1940, and his successor, Alan Brooke, considered that road blocks hindered the defenders more than they would a potential attacker, and most obstacles were removed.

Two obstructions described as 'stone blockhouses' were built at Neston Cross and at the 'Cockpit' (at the top of Buggen Lane). When they were broken up, the Home Guard could not find the means of removing the debris, so the council did it, in May 1941. They also removed four-foot concrete sewer pipes which had been positioned to block Parkgate Road at its junction with Church Lane.

The fear of airborne invasion, unlikely though that was in the North-West, made it necessary to obstruct the possible landing places for planes or gliders. In Raby, the farmers were required to place obstacles such as farm machinery in the middle of large fields, while in Parkgate Arthur Draper saw zigzag trenches dug across part of Parks Field.

Another form of defence that appeared locally was the pillbox. These were concrete machine-gun emplacements, like small forts, first used in 1917 by the Germans, who made them circular, whence the nickname 'pillbox'. Along the south and east coasts of England where invasion could be expected, pillboxes formed part of defensive lines and were usually positioned in sight of each other. There seem to have been no such defensive lines planned for the North-West: although the Lancashire coast had a defensive system, North Wales, the Dee shores and Wirral did

Chapter Six

not. But there were some scattered pillboxes built locally, for Ironside had recommended that local councils should prepare their own defences because it was *"stupid to repair roads, trim hedges and grass, when pillboxes are needed"*.

Perhaps 25,000 pillboxes were built throughout Britain. How many were built in Wirral is not known, but seven remain: one near Caldy crossroads, one at Brimstage, two at Port Sunlight, two at Childer Thornton and one at Parkgate. There used to be one by the marsh at Denhall and one at Ledsham. Pillbox designs were issued by the Fortifications and Works Department of the War Office. There were six basic plans, which were modified by local contractors, like Fleming or Norman in Neston, to suit the terrain. The Parkgate pillbox is a reduced and irregular version of Type FW3/24, a hexagonal plan with one longer side. It has seven loopholes, including one on either side of the door in the long side. The design was intended for six men, potentially armed with five bren-guns

The Home Guard supplied the labour for construction of the pillbox in Station Road, Parkgate. The open aspect of the site is apparent in this picture.

(light machine-guns) and one rifle, although the chance that a Home Guard unit would have five brens, if any, was remote.

Arnold Whiteway worked for Fleming's as a joiner, and helped to build several pillboxes, at Hoylake, Thurstaston and Ledsham. They assembled wooden shuttering in the workshop, and at the site laid a thick concrete base with wire reinforcement, and constructed the walls of concrete poured between the shuttering. The roof would be twelve inches or more in thickness. One pillbox would take six men about three weeks to build. Mr Whiteway did not himself work on the Parkgate pillbox, but it is known that the Home Guard supplied the labour for it. These random pillboxes may chiefly have been intended to bolster civilian morale, but apart from that the probable reason for the Parkgate one was to defend the railway bridge, and perhaps to make time for it to be blown up by our own troops to prevent the enemy using it.

Another local initiative was the construction of rifle slits on top of the sea wall beside the Old Quay House, probably by the Home Guard to counter any airborne landing on the estuary. The derelict Old Quay House itself was blown up early in the war by troops as a demolition exercise.

The danger to Liverpool and Merseyside was not from invasion, but from bombers. Against the bombers there were three forms of defence: to attack them with fighters; to harass them from the ground with anti-aircraft guns, assisted by searchlights and barrage balloons; and to persuade them to drop their bombs harmlessly on decoy targets, a system codenamed Starfish.

Fighter aircraft were in short supply, and the military planners assumed that they would be mostly needed to defend the south and east coasts of the country. Therefore Liverpool was designated a 'gun-defended area' using the Royal Artillery's Heavy Anti-Aircraft guns, known as HAA. Although there were some fighters in our area, chiefly for training, it was obviously dangerous for them to tackle bombers which were being fired at from the ground at the same time. In addition, bombers attacked Merseyside almost wholly at night, when our fighters were ineffective until fitted with radar, which happened only when the attacks on Liverpool had virtually ceased. It was the noise of our own guns, therefore, which disturbed the nights of Neston people and made them feel directly involved in the blitz of Merseyside. Those living nearer the centre of Wirral, like David Woodhouse at Willaston, had a more dramatic view:

If you went out at night, you could see searchlight beams from all directions. I could see shells bursting. Ships in the docks and the Mersey fired their pom-pom guns and there were continuous flashes in the sky.

At the end of 1940 there were 56 HAA guns defending Merseyside, but the Battle of the Atlantic increased the strategic importance of Liverpool, so that by May 1941 120 guns were in position. There were two HAA batteries near Neston, at Raby and Puddington, and these will be described. There were other batteries at Thurstaston, Bidston, Ince and Upton by Chester. These were fixed guns, but mobile guns were also used, moving from place to place to encourage the civilians and confuse the enemy. These mobile guns (or perhaps the same gun seen in different places) were Bofors guns. Hugh Norman saw one being set up on the village green in Little Neston, with a clip of five shells on the side of the gun. He also saw the gun operate on a patch of waste ground at the corner of Victoria Road and Woodfall Lane. One of the Guernsey evacuees reported that a mobile gun, firing beside Neston Institute, made the windows rattle, and another witness saw one at Parkgate near the pillbox.

During air raids, Neston people could see searchlights piercing the darkness in search of targets for the guns. Each site would have had one 90-inch or 150-inch searchlight with a generator and sound locator, manned by a sergeant and eleven men. There were searchlights at Puddington, Willaston near the mill, Hooton, Ledsham, Burton Point and Parkgate. For the Parkgate searchlight, the Army first requisitioned a field off Bevyl Road, but then preferred a site in Boathouse Lane opposite the turning to Wood Lane. Arthur Draper saw the soldiers there, living in camouflaged bell tents, although these may later have been replaced by huts. He also saw that the site was defended by small guns in sandbagged emplacements.

Both the Raby and the Puddington HAA batteries used a radar location system introduced early in the war. The course of the plane was traced on a glass screen which enabled its speed over the ground to be measured. A plotting officer could then work out a point of interception with a ruler scaled for speed, reading off the gunnery data with the help of range tables. The radar used wire mesh nets 85 yards in diameter, constructed around the receiver cabin. Graham Langley saw this at Raby:

The field below the camp on Mr Griffiths' farm had a thick wire netting mesh stretched over hundreds of angle-iron posts placed so that it was dead level. In the centre was a revolving square cabin containing the radar apparatus. Later an improved version, not needing the wire matting, was put in one of our own fields.

At both Raby and Puddington there were probably five officers including one female ATS officer, 69 men and 102 women. The ATS women manned the radar and predictor equipment, but it was maintained by civilian electrical engineers, who were later drafted into REME. The men were partly Royal Artillery soldiers and partly Home Guard.

The purpose of both batteries of four guns each, so George Langley was told when some officers arrived on his land at Willow Brow Farm, Raby, to choose a site, was to harass enemy planes which were escaping from Liverpool over mid-Wirral. The next day, 30 September 1940, the troops arrived in four buses. They set up a tented camp on low, damp ground where there was some tree cover, and the next day four 3-inch guns arrived and were pulled onto the field by the tractor of the neighbouring farmer, Mr Leach. The ground soon became a quagmire, with the troops floundering about in the mud.

We had been allowed to leave a free-range hen house on the field, but one evening a soldier, returning the worse for wear from the Wheatsheaf, wrung the necks of some hens and threw the heads through the flap of the sergeant's tent. Next day we were compensated and we moved the hens.

Some ten days later it was decided to replace the 3-inch guns with larger, 3.7-inch, weapons. But the tractor driver, faced with a difficult entry to the field, ended up in a potato clamp trench, where he stuck. Next morning early a captain and lieutenant knocked on our front door to apologize to father and explained they had decided to decamp into a field at the back of our farm where they had parked the guns overnight, as it was a far better site.

George Langley was immensely relieved to hear this, as he had thought he might lose half his farm, but the chosen field belonged to Mr Leach, who was not amused and withdrew his offers of help with transport.

The new camp was set up with wooden and corrugated-iron Nissen huts, roadways, cook-house, male and female quarters, a NAAFI and toilets with filter beds. The site itself was defended from ground attack with a Bofors gun and three machine-guns.

It was difficult to know whether anti-aircraft fire actually brought down any German planes. David Woodhouse remembered that the Raby battery was awarded a barrel of beer by the landlord of the Wheatsheaf when they were told they had shot down an enemy bomber.

Robert Hook used to take details of the recognition colours of British aircraft to both gun sites.

> *Details of the colours of the day were delivered in envelopes. I went by car or on a motorbike. The unit at Raby was from the 93rd Regiment TA. There was an Ordnance depot at Arrowe Park, and ammunition was taken from there to the battery in a truck.*

The Raby camp closed in March 1945, when George Langley wrote in his diary, "*Camp gone and no more pig swill*"; however, in June and October he reported that some soldiers had returned. These were squatters with their families, but the council moved them out as the huts were not fit for permanent habitation. The Nissen huts were finally dismantled in January 1947, though this was not the end of the story. In 1961 a Royal Observer Corps station was moved from Bromborough to Raby, and an underground nuclear bunker was built where the camp had been. This bunker remained operational until the end of the Cold War.

More detailed information is available about the Royal Artillery units which manned the Puddington guns. In March 1941 289 Battery of the

Part of the anti-aircraft gunsite at Puddington, as it is today. The undergrowth and trees have grown up in the last fifty years, since the site was abandoned.

The Defences

This and other shell racks still survive at the Puddington anti-aircraft gunsite.

93rd HAA Regiment was preparing the site, codenamed YY and later H21. Four 3.7-inch guns and their equipment arrived on 13 March. Only ten days later a new unit, 319 Battery, took over. Harry Welch worked at Bibby's Home Farm and saw the soldiers come: *"When they first came they slept under hedges. Then they built huts in sections like hen houses, with the officers in one of Bibby's cottages."*

In April 1942 another unit, 476 Mixed Battery (of 149 Mixed HAA Regiment) took over the site, by which time its four guns were 4.5 inch, with their shells stored in racks in concrete sections next to them. There was yet another change of unit in January 1943, when 616 Mixed Battery took over. One of the ATS girls in this battery was Flo Hassall, aged 18:

I worked in the plotting room, which was underground behind the guns. There was a board and the direction of the planes was plotted on it. The officers worked out from the instruments the height and range of the planes. They had earphones to the men on the guns to give the co-ordinates of the target. The German planes followed the river at night and the guns were manned all the time. We were very angry when enemy planes were coming in. There was a

Chapter Six

sense of urgency when the alarm bell sounded, and we were very much on edge to try to stop them or divert them to drop their bombs in the river or countryside. I had seen the destruction that bombing had done in Birmingham.

Harry Welch recalled that the cottages by the farm shook when the guns were fired.

There was relaxation as well. There was a rest room in a Nissen hut by the control room and on Saturdays there were dances in the dining room. Local people also came, and Flo Hughes met her husband at a dance. They also went to the village hall in Burton for concerts. Nancy Sowden went several times to sing to the soldiers and was paid five shillings on each occasion.

When the Army left Puddington they held a final social evening: *"They gave us a good do before they went."* Bill Pye, son of Bibby's farm manager, remembered the radar matting: *"When the Army had gone we played on the wire netting. It was like a giant trampoline."* His father offered him £5 to clear away the rusting barbed wire that remained, and it took him two weeks to do the job.

As at Raby, squatters moved into the empty huts, but they stayed much longer. Mrs Muriel Jones was one of them:

I was living with my in-laws as my husband was in the forces and friends said the huts were empty. I thought, if I moved in, I could get a council house more quickly, but it was many years before we did. The huts were open with a stove in the centre, but Cheshire County Council took over and provided partitions. We had two bedrooms and a dining room, and there was already a back kitchen with a sink. We paid 7s. 6d. a week rent. There was no means of heating water so we had to boil it. It was my own place with my own front door. The floors were concrete so I bought roofing felt to cover them. I polished it with floor polish and it came up well. We left in 1951 and there were still quite a few people there.

Another way of harassing the bombers was the barrage balloon. These were huge grey bags of rubberized cotton, 63 by 31 feet in size, filled with 19,000 cubic feet of gas, and tethered by long steel cables. Their purpose was to force planes to fly above the balloons to avoid hitting the cables, thus making bomb aiming more difficult and preventing dive bombing. Balloon sites were maintained by the RAF and, although there was none in the Neston area, the balloons could be seen floating over Birkenhead. If they broke loose they could be a nuisance, especially if the cable trailed over rooftops. When a loose balloon floated over Willow Brow Farm in

The Defences

Raby, all the poultry hid. Another balloon came down in a field at Goldstraw Farm, Ness, in January 1941. *"The whole staff turned out to capture it and were nearly frozen."* The next day fifteen engineers took it away. When Harry Welch saw a stray balloon drift by his front door, *"we thought the Germans had come."*

Another way of protecting the bombers' real targets was to set up decoy targets. This system of dummy targets, codenamed Starfish, was intended to deceive the enemy into dropping their bombs in harmless places. There were three such targets on the Wirral shore of the Dee.

The furthest was on the Middle Eye of Hilbre Islands. There was a generator on the main island, so that the decoy lights could be lit when a raid was expected. There was another Starfish target on the golf course of Heswall Golf Club, beyond the northern end of Parkgate. Arthur Draper used to play among a system of lights there. Mrs Crook recorded that some people thought that this decoy was altogether too close to Parkgate. The third local decoy target was on the marsh at Burton, described as a dummy runway, upstream of Taylor's Gutter.

> *Just before the raids began, the Army covered about a square mile, from the Broad Brook towards the Welsh hills, back down towards Summers' steelworks and in towards Denhall Lane, with a network of scaffold tubes with electric lights suspended from them. This was known as the decoy, and this area was honoured nightly with incendiary bombs. The decoy did its job well. I can remember the Army lads doing their maintenance and inspection work, travelling round on a tracked railway buggy.*

The form of defence that involved local people most closely was the Home Guard. *"It was not like those silly beggars on television,"* said George Tilley, *"there was no messing about. They were all dedicated men."* The Home Guard was initiated by a broadcast, on 14 May 1940, by Anthony Eden, the Secretary of State for War. He said,

> *I want to speak to you tonight about the form of warfare which the Germans have been employing so successfully against Holland and Belgium, namely the dropping of troops by parachute behind the main defence lines. We want large numbers of men who are British subjects, between the ages of 17 and 65, to come forward now and offer their services.*

A quarter of a million men enrolled within 24 hours of the broadcast. *"I went to the police station and joined the same day"*, said Eddie Evans. *"They just wrote down my name and address and I went home."* The force was called the Local Defence Volunteers at first, but two months later, at Churchill's insistence, the name was changed to the Home Guard. A meeting at Heswall, ten days after Eden's broadcast, was addressed by Major Cecil Marsden, MC, at which enrolment forms and LDV armbands were issued to 3,348 men who had already volunteered. They formed the Wirral Group, commanded by Marsden, and this was divided into four battalions. No.5 Battalion, which included Neston, was commanded by Captain Aled Roberts of Sutton Hall, Little Sutton. Commissions were first issued to the Home Guard in February 1941, and the battalions were renumbered so that Neston was included in the 20th Battalion, and Wirral Group, still with four battalions, was called No.5 Sector.

Officers of No.5 Sector (Wirral Group) Home Guard, probably in December 1944, when the Home Guard was stood down. *L. to r: standing*, Not Known, Capt. Porter, NK, NK, Capt. Harold Alexander, Capt. Craig, Capt. Walter Plummer; *seated*, Capt. Mather, Maj. Geoffrey Boston, Maj. Glasspool, Col. Cecil Marsden, MC (commanding), NK (officer from the Regular Army), Maj. Harrison, Capt. William Walker, MC (adjutant).

The 20th Battalion was split into several companies, G Company being the Neston one, commanded by Captain Rennie. Within G Company

The Defences

there were three platoons. The Neston platoon was commanded by Kenneth Montgomery; the Little Neston platoon was commanded by John Hassall, assisted by M. A. M. Dillon and later by Jack Henderson; and the Burton platoon was commanded by Walter Plummer (whose brother Edward was the chief ARP warden).

Neston Home Guard platoon, December 1944. L. to r: *back row*, Jim Mathews, Not Known, Tom Tilston, Ernest Jellicoe, NK, Charles Seymour, NK, Roy Cameron, NK, NK, Matthew Leonard, Bill Parry, Ted Gunning; *middle row*, Jack Minshell, Steve Scarrett, Walter Main, George Pearson, (?) Pierce, George Fairhurst, (?) Partridge, Charlie Jellicoe, Laurence Whitter, Tom Peers, Jack Parr, Harry Foote, NK; *front row*, Joe Mealor, NK, Jim Bromilow, George Lee, Frank Hope, Kenneth Montgomery (CO), Bill Jackson, (?) Webster, Billy Cotterell, Frankie Dolan, Walter Mosedale.

Eddie Scott joined the Little Neston platoon:

At that time I was a schoolboy of 17 and the parental permission necessary before I could join was not forthcoming for a few weeks, until it became clear that the LDV was not to be a comic, ragtime body as portrayed years later in the Dad's Army TV series. Our uniforms were whatever we stood up in, with khaki LDV armbands. Some brought shotguns and birdshot cartridges, and some bright spark taught us to take out the end wad from a cartridge, pour out the lead shot, half-fill the cavity with molten candle wax and pour back the shot. Fired from a 12-bore shotgun, this missile would pass through a four-inch railway sleeper at 25 yards. Other volunteers had to make do with hedging slashers, pitchforks or even wooden staves.

Quite soon, however, American .300 P14 rifles arrived, in the packing cases in which they had been stored in grease since 1918, and our first task was to clean

Chapter Six

Little Neston Home Guard platoon, December 1944. L. to r: *back row*, John Phillips, Frank Norman, (George Grimshaw?), Alf Hand, Sam Smith, (?) Crellin; *middle row*, Jim Bartley, Bert Henderson, Alf Bailey, Charlie Lee, Bill Jones, Jim Iddon; *front row*, Donald Milne, George Worthington, Jack Henderson (2nd in command), John Hassall (commanding), Morris Hall, John Roberts.

one apiece. A regular sergeant from a nearby unit taught us how to use them. After each training session we took our rifles home with us in case the invasion happened at night.

Within a few months articles of uniform began to appear in dribs and drabs: battledress with Home Guard shoulder flashes, boots and forage caps with Cheshire Regiment cap badges.

My own job was as one of a six-man section to guard the reservoir for about one night a week. Stationed in a garden shed furnished with a couple of double bunks and a Tilley lamp, we patrolled the perimeter in pairs for two hours at a time with four hours off. As a mere schoolboy I counted myself blessed with my section companions, two of whom were muscular to the point of being cubic: plumber Eddie Evans, an international gymnast, and Jim Idden, an amateur boxer and ABA finalist. In this company I felt quite safe.

The Defences

Members of the local Home Guard, displaying (*middle row, centre*) a trophy probably won in a recent competition.

Eddie Evans rose to the occasion when a bomb fell on the nearby railway line:

We went across the field and cows chased us because they were frightened. We had to fix our bayonets to keep them off. We could not get over the barbed wire fence because of our baggy trousers. The cows pushed at us and eventually we got over.

The threat of invasion seemed very real when the *Luftwaffe* launched a massive attack on RAF airfields in the Battle of Britain. On 7 September 1940 a telephone message was sent at 11 p.m. to all Home Guard units to stand to. The intention of GHQ Home Forces was to alert the south and east coasts only, because tidal conditions were suitable for an invasion, and the message was passed to other areas in error. When George Tilley answered this call,

I went to Burton to stand guard by the school. I took my brother-in-law on the back step of my bicycle. We had between us one rifle and five rounds of ammunition. They were expecting German paratroops. We stayed that night until daylight.

Hugh Whittemore, a Ness farmer, and his companion, Joe Waring, a milkman who had a float pony, spent that night patrolling on horseback. When Frank Latham told his father that *"we have been invaded"*, his father's only comment was that it could not be true because no one had rung the church bells, and he went to sleep again.

Chapter Six

The Little Neston platoon used to practise with their rifles on the Sealand firing range, and they learned how to use hand grenades. They made Molotov cocktails (beer bottles filled with petrol) to use against tanks, and eventually received a real anti-tank weapon, a PIAT mortar, which looked like a piece of drainpipe. They learned fieldcraft:

> *In these exercises my Calday [Grange School] chum Ron Benbow and I were appointed scouts. Our task was to move ahead of the main body, locate the enemy and report back. To get information back without becoming an umpire's casualty, we learned to 'run' on elbows and toecaps. But we found that we could not see where we were going and a signalling system was needed. Ron and I had both learned Morse at Calday, and Hugh Whittemore set up a communications room at his farm where we practised on Morse equipment, and we also used semaphore flags and Aldis lamps.*

One memorable exercise, with other units, was a night attack on the Royal Ordnance depot at Capenhurst to test their defences. Eddie Scott was in the main party:

> *At about 20.00 hours we assembled at White House platoon headquarters and were issued with blank rifle ammunition. We marched along the High Road and then proceeded stealthily across the fields until we reached the chain-link fence surrounding the depot. We were spread out along the fence, in prone firing positions awaiting orders, when hell and rifle fire broke out all round. Searchlights flashed and whistles blew. It appeared that the depot defence force had not been warned of an exercise attack. It was fortunate there were no casualties.*

William Hough was also there, with rather different memories:

> *Joe Oxton liked his ale and he had been in the Royal Oak. He had about eight pints and I helped to look after him. He was jolly, not legless. We went straight to Capenhurst and arrived half an hour before the others. Joe knew how to get in as he had worked there as a bricklayer. The place was guarded by regular soldiers. We ambled round inside for a bit and then Joe went up to one of the soldiers and said, 'All reet, owd'un, we're the Neston Home Guard.' The soldiers were very angry and we were taken to the main gate. Later on Jack Henderson, one of our officers, had to come and vouch for us. The soldiers had thought we were possible fifth-columnists. Jack, you could tell, was very proud of us as we had met the objective. I was made leader of the assault group and given a Thompson sub-machine-gun and 300 rounds of ammunition to take home with me.*

When he was recently shown the entry about himself in the Home Guard register, he realized that he had added a year to his age to gain entry.

Frank Latham was in the Burton platoon:

> *I was a teenager, but most were older men, including Gerard Biggs, a roadsweeper who seemed over 70 years old, and Major Higgin of Puddington, who was a private like me. I think we met once a week and often on Sundays for weapon training with mock battles in the woods.*

One task given to the Home Guard in the early days was to check identity cards at road blocks, a task which Bill Sleigh found boring, as *"there were very few cars and only two buses."* Charlie Swift was checking people's papers at the waterworks in Lees Lane when an Irishman, who had been drinking at the Nag's Head in Willaston, came by on a bike. He was stopped by the Home Guard, but fell off the bike and they could not get him on again. They covered him with a groundsheet and left him by the side of the road to sober up. Later on, a young couple came along in a car. When they were asked for their papers, the man refused to hand them over, possibly because he was with someone else's wife. The Home Guard said, "If you don't hand over your papers, we'll shoot you." The man replied, "You haven't got the guts to do that." The Home Guard simply pointed to the man lying by the side of the road, covered in a sheet, and the driver handed over his papers very quickly.

No wonder that Eddie Scott said, when called up in January 1942, *"I left the Home Guard for the relative safety and sanity of the Royal Signals."*

In July 1942 the headquarters of No.5 Sector Home Guard, which included the 20th Battalion and G (Neston) Company, moved to Neston. Part of the headquarters had been housed in G. S. Boston's stables at Hadlow Wood, Willaston, because Boston was Col. Marsden's staff officer. In 1942 the army requisitioned The Mount, Hinderton, on the High Road, and this became the new headquarters, with a flat for the adjutant, William Walker, MC.

The strength of the 20th Cheshire Battalion was 858 on formation, rising to a peak of 1,211, and 860 at stand-down. The full battalion paraded together only four times: three times at Little Sutton and once at Neston in 1943. There was only one full battalion camp, at Sealand in 1942, but frequent weekend camps, often at a disused gun site at Ledsham. According to its historian, *"The battalion seems to have been independent minded and tried to avoid interference from the plethora of senior officers."* Numbers tended to dwindle as the younger men were called up. The

Chapter Six

> **I**n the years when our Country
>
> was in mortal danger
>
> GEOFFREY SHAKERLEY BOSTON
>
> who served 16th, June, 1940 – 31st, December, 1944
>
> gave generously of his time and
>
> powers to make himself ready
>
> for her defence by force of arms
>
> and with his life if need be.
>
> *George R.I.*
>
> # THE HOME GUARD

Members of the Home Guard received certificates, too.

The Defences

Little Neston platoon register lists 137 names; 64 remained at the end, 41 having been called up, 8 declared medically unfit and 24 having left for various reasons.

The Home Guard was stood down on 31 December 1944.

SOURCES

This chapter was written by Edward Hilditch.

Publications and other records consulted were Brigadier N. W. Routledge, *History of the Royal Regiment of Artillery, Anti-aircraft Artillery 1914-1955* (1994); the war diaries of units stationed at Puddington; the records of Neston Urban District Council; Henry Wills, *Pillboxes, a Study of UK Defences* (1985); and *The History of the Cheshire Home Guard* (1950).

Information was also provided by the Royal Artillery Historical Trust.

And we thank Reg Bushell, Marie Crook, Arthur Draper, Eddie Evans, Colin Foote, Flo Hassall, Robert Hook, William Hough, Bill Jones, Muriel Jones, George Langley, Graham Langley, Frank Latham, Dr Lewis McAfee, Hugh Norman, Bill Pye, Eddie Scott, Bill Sleigh, Nancy Sowden, Charlie Swift, George Tilley, Arnold Whiteway, Hugh Whittemore and David Woodhouse for their memories.

CHAPTER SEVEN

FOOD

Food was on everybody's mind during the war. When Hitler failed to gain aerial superiority in the Battle of Britain and so could not invade, his strategy was to force Britain to her knees by an economic blockade. German submarines had begun their attack on our shipping immediately war was declared in 1939.

For this the country was well prepared. Ration books had been ready since 1938; they were issued in October 1939 as soon as national registration had taken place, and rationing started the following January. The rationed goods were distributed to shops according to the number of their customers, so every household had to register with a particular shop for the basic foodstuffs. In Neston, for example, Anne Gray's mother registered with Irwin's for groceries, with Barnes' for meat and with Nicholls' for milk. There was a choice: groceries were also sold by Pearson's, Hughes' and the Co-op, meat was sold by Pyke's, Swift's and the British & Argentine Meat Company, and milk by Harold Quarmby, but once registered with a particular supplier it was difficult to change. All this was administered, on behalf of the Ministry of Food, by Neston Food Office.

F. R. Poole, the Town Clerk, was the Food Executive Officer, and he headed the Neston Food Control Committee, with five councillors, five consumer representatives, and several trade members, including W. Irving (baker), W. K. Nicholls (dairyman) and George Pearson (grocer). He had owl-like horn-rimmed glasses, and was always dressed in pin stripes, black coat and bowler hat and carried a tightly rolled umbrella. It was in the name of this committee that Frank Poole established a food office at Woodhill, Earle Drive, on the corner with Wood Lane. The house had been used as a small private school, but this moved to the house next door. There was a staff of two men, Mr Craig and Mr J. H. Williams, and four women, including Mary Chrimes, who had been working at the town hall and transferred to the food office on 9 October 1939.

Mr Williams was a retired headmaster and was over 65 when he started work at the food office that September. He looked like Winston Churchill, and people often commented on the likeness. People thought that Mr Craig looked like Ramsay Macdonald. No one came to teach us: we had to pick things up as we went along.

Their first task was to tour the district issuing ration books, in Willaston, Burton, Little Neston and Parkgate. *"The WVS assisted in driving us to these places. One lady took us in her car and we were petrified we would not get there as she was such a bad driver. Mr Poole also took us in his car."*

The actual rations allowed varied from time to time, but rationing reached its peak in August 1942 after the fall of Singapore had put extra strain on our food supplies. There was a weekly ration of meat, bacon, sugar, fats and cheese, and a monthly ration of soap, jam, dried eggs, sweets and chocolate. Milk and shell eggs were controlled, but varied with the season. As examples of the quantities allowed, each person could buy roughly a pound of meat a week and half a pound each of sugar, fats and cheese. Some other foods, mainly tinned, were 'on points': each person had twenty points a month to use as they liked, or could find the goods. Bread, potatoes, fish, poultry, fruit and vegetables were not rationed. Free or cheap milk was provided for children, and orange juice and cod liver oil for babies under two. Rationing was accepted as fair and necessary, but one's entitlement was by no means always available, particularly of meat. As Miss Barber recalled, *"It was tight but you managed."* Kathleen Gray had a vivid memory of the day that sweet rationing was introduced. She travelled each day to school from Parkgate station, and on that morning Herbert Stewart, the station master, emptied the platform machines and gave the chocolate to the children on the train.

Frank Poole was Town Clerk of Neston, but also Billeting Officer, Food Executive Officer, Local Fuel Overseer, etc.

Retailers cut the coupons out of the books as they supplied their customers, and each month they sent in their coupons to the food office. We issued permits to the value of goods sold, which they could take to the wholesalers to replenish their stocks.

Food

The main task of the food office was to regulate the ration books.

When books were finished people had to fill in the back page and then we could issue a new book. The back page formed our record, which we had to keep on file. If people lost a book they had to apply to us for a new one. Temporary cards had to be issued when people were going away. Before the children at Mostyn

A familiar and essential document during the war, the ration book continued in use, though for a dwindling number of foodstuffs, until 1954.

House went home for their holidays, someone had to bring in a whole pile of books for us to issue temporary cards.

A few people could not cope with ration books. Neston then had two 'drop-out' characters called Tim and Blossom: *"They came in each week for temporary cards. Their manner of existence meant they could not look after a book, so we made sure they had enough coupons for a week at a time."*

When people got married, they wanted ration books in their new name at once before they went away. The food office demanded the marriage certificate before issuing a new book.

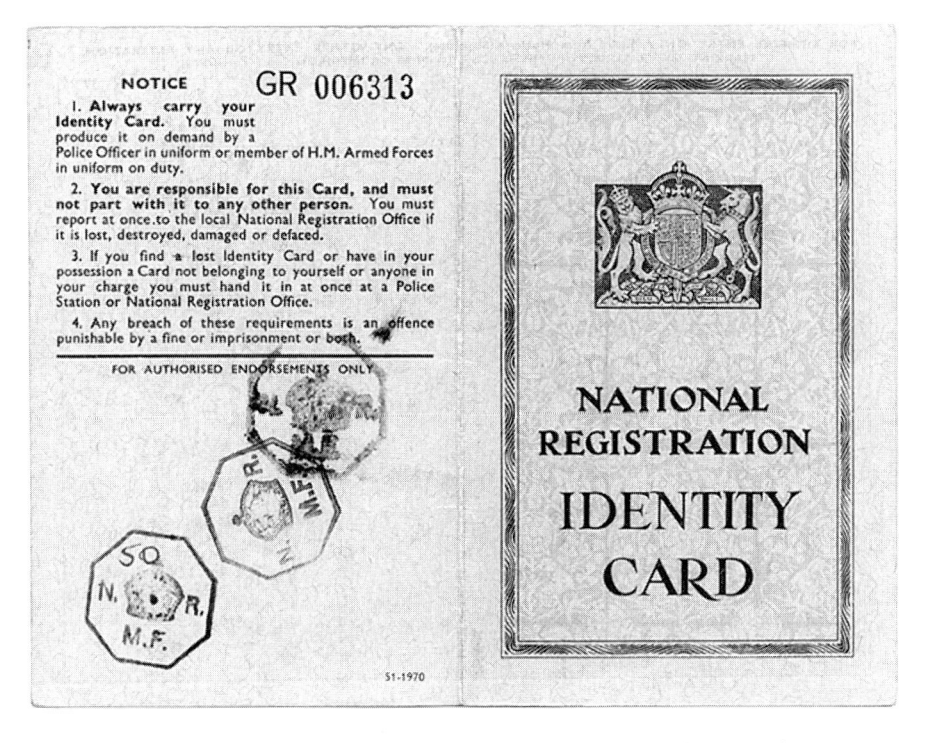

Identity cards were important wartime documents, to be carried by everyone at all times.

The food office had many other duties, including the issue of identity cards, providing extra coupons for people entitled to extra rations, for medical reasons such as pregnancy, or for heavy workers such as the Parkgate fishermen and farm workers. Extra sugar rations could be claimed by beekeepers and jam makers. The Neston Food Control Committee was also responsible for issuing catering licences, which enabled restaurants, canteens and residential establishments like Mostyn House to buy food in bulk. Another of Frank Poole's titles was Local Fuel Overseer, and the food office at Woodhill issued licences to buy fuel. They also issued clothing coupons.

The public were encouraged to grow their own vegetables, and an official campaign called 'Dig for Victory' was launched. In October 1939 Frank Poole advertised that Neston Council had acquired some land, under the Cultivation of Land (Allotments) Order, and applications for allotments were invited. The Neston Council of Social Service already had some fifty allotments beside Burton Road, next to the former brickworks on the corner with Marshlands Road. It also held a piece of land beside Neston's New Cinema which the owner, J. F. Burns, leased to it for £1 a year, which he returned as a subscription. In 1940 Burns leased the cinema, but not the NCSS plot, to Paramount Picture Theatres for 21 years. Neston Council set up allotments in various places over the next two years: for example, its tenants in Mostyn Gardens, Parkgate, were offered allotments at one shilling a year. The tenants were issued with a long list of rules, the chief being that only vegetables and food crops could be grown. In November 1942 the Ministry of Agriculture appealed to local authorities to find as much land as possible for allotments.

The NCSS included an Allotment Association, affiliated to the London-based 'Allotment Gardens for the Unemployed', which supplied seeds, potatoes, fertilizer, spades and forks to members. It agreed that, in the circumstance of war, it would supply allotment holders who were employed as well as the unemployed. On its own account, the NCSS Allotment Association bought lime for its members and then claimed half the cost from the Ministry of Agriculture. But the price was controlled and the Ministry knocked part of the cost off both the lime and the transport charge. The supplier had to refund the excess.

Farming was strictly controlled by War Agricultural Executive Committees, known as War Ags, in each county. The War Ag for Cheshire was based at Reaseheath Agricultural College near Nantwich. They made a survey of every farm, reporting on the condition of the buildings, fences, roads and drains, as well as the land, and if necessary on the suitability of the farmer. They could order which crops were to be grown and could dispossess farmers who disobeyed or were incompetent. An example of their orders is a directive, dated 6 December 1941, to W. Swift to plough an eight-acre field of permanent grassland at the top of Bevyl Road, Parkgate, and to plant oats on it. He was also directed to plant twelve acres with wheat, one acre with potatoes and three acres with forage crops. Under a similar order, Geoff Nicholls of Ashfield Farm had to plough Parks Field in Parkgate, probably for the first time ever. He found it very difficult to plough, but it yielded a fine crop. The War Ag people came to Willow Brow Farm, Raby, on 2 October 1939 *"to see how many acres of old pasture I was going to plough up"*. Three hundred acres of the inner marsh near Puddington, known as Palethorpe's Bog (because it had been used by Palethorpe's Foods as a duck shoot), was drained to provide water for Summers' steelworks, and then reclaimed for potato crops by Karl Jennings with the War Ag's help.

Karl Jennings, who came to Ashfield Hall Farm, across the Chester High Road from Geoff Nicholls, in 1942, found the War Ag very helpful:

> *The farm was completely unproductive: parkland, and neglected at that. In the first year I cultivated twenty acres for market garden crops. This was important for the firm's business (potato and produce wholesalers) and for the war effort. Afterwards I took over all 214 acres, run as a mixed farm: cattle, cereals grown for animal feed and mostly potatoes. I worked closely with the War Agricultural Committee for advice in new methods, new modern machinery and modern cattle management, all this for greatest efficiency and maximum output.*

One of the effects of the War Ags was to increase the number of tractors on British farms by nearly four times.

At the start of the war Geoff Nicholls was farming some of the land of Ashfield Hall Farm across the road from his own. At that time there were soldiers, Royal Artillery, billeted in the hall, so he took care to ensure his men kept all gates closed. One night the soldiers left a gate open and cattle strayed onto the Chester High Road. In the blackout an approaching car driver failed to see Mr Nicholls flagging him down, and hit a cow and killed it. When Mr Nicholls went to report this, the commanding officer at the hall said that the King never admitted liability, but *"you are dealing with gentlemen"*. Nothing happened, however, until a solicitor was called in and extracted compensation.

One hazard for farmers in March 1941 was an outbreak of foot and mouth disease, necessitating the slaughter of many cattle and sheep. John Pye, the manager of Bibby's Home Farm at Puddington, journeyed to Scotland to buy replacements. One of the cows was said to have come from the field near Glasgow where Rudolf Hess, Hitler's deputy, had landed by parachute. The cow was known at Puddington as Miss Hess.

COPY FOR LANDLORD.	5338 / 1473

CHESHIRE WAR AGRICULTURAL EXECUTIVE COMMITTEE.
REASEHEATH, NANTWICH.

DEFENCE REGULATIONS 1939.
THE CULTIVATION OF LANDS ORDER 1939.

To Mr. C.G.Nicholls, of Ashfield Farm, Neston, Wirral in the County of Chester or other the occupier of the land described in the schedules hereto. The Cheshire War Agricultural Executive Committee being the body authorised to exercise on behalf of the Minister of Agriculture and Fisheries within the administrative County of Chester the powers in that behalf conferred by Regulation 62 (1) of the Defence Regulations 1939, hereby direct you to carry out in respect of the land described in the Schedules hereto the works of cultivation specified in the said Schedules.

Failure to comply with these directions or any part thereof is an offence under the Defence Regulations.

By order of the Committee,

Date **23rd January 1941**

W. B. MERCER,
Executive Officer.

THE FIRST SCHEDULE.

DISTRICT	PARISH	ORDNANCE MAP NO. AND EDN.	ACREAGE	DESCRIPTION	REQUIRED CULTIVATION
Wirral	**Neston**	461 (1913)	6.643	Perm Grass	Plough before **15th Feb** 1941, apply ----- cwts. per acre of and carry out all operations necessary to produce a crop of **OATS** to be harvested in 1941.

DISTRICT	PARISH	ORDNANCE MAP NO. AND EDN.	ACREAGE	DESCRIPTION	REQUIRED CULTIVATION
					Plough before 1941, apply cwts. per acre of and carry out all operations necessary to produce a crop of to be harvested in 1941.

THE SECOND SCHEDULE.
On the holding named above grow and harvest in 1941 at least ------ acres of POTATOES, including any specified on this or any previous Direction.

THE THIRD SCHEDULE.
On the holding named above grow in 1941 and harvest in the winter of 1941/42 at least **12½** acres of Root or Green forage crops (excluding potatoes) including any specified on this or any previous Direction.

PLEASE TURN OVER

Name and address of Landlord or Agent: Messrs.Baird, Smith & Grimes, 71, Lord Street.Liverpool. Neston U.D.C. - Town Hall - High Street - Neston cum Parkgate.

An order, issued by the Cheshire War Ag in 1941 to Geoff Nicholls, to plough up permanent grassland for oats, and also to grow 12fi acres of root or green forage crops.

Prices were controlled from 1940. On 11 February of that year, George Langley of Raby *"took two calves to Hooton* [livestock market], *the first lot under the Food Control."* Similarly, produce had to be reported: *"Sent in potato form to Ministry of Food, 34 tons."* Almost at the end of the war, in March 1945, Langley recorded, *"Killed a pig, butcher from Willaston killed it, had to surrender 52 bacon coupons for it."* The farm had a licence to kill two pigs a year for their own use. Langley also applied for a licence to sell eggs, but the Bebington food office would not grant it.

In 1941 Liverpool University's Faculty of Veterinary Science opened its research station at Leahurst on the Chester High Road, previously a private house. The aim was *"to improve the clinical education of veterinary students in farm animals as a vital contribution to the provision of food in wartime"*. The site was chosen with the help of J. P. Bibby, who lived next door, because the students could use the two experimental farms belonging to J. Bibby & Sons, at Hanns Hall, Willaston, and Home Farm, Puddington.

It was not just humans whose food was rationed. In January 1941 the Ministry of Agriculture and Fisheries announced that *"the Government has decided that it is now necessary to introduce a general rationing scheme for livestock"*, and explained that the War Ags had to work out the details. In March that year George Langley *"went to Reaseheath for ration coupons for cattle."* Coupons for protein and cereals were issued for three months and had to be deposited with the merchants that the farmer had registered with. The next winter, after farmers had been urged to grow their own forage crops, and in view of limited supplies, the scheme was tightened: *"Farmers are expected to have become largely self-supporting."* In October 1941 A. M. D. Grenfell obtained a ration card for an 'urban horse'.

Most schools cultivated some land and grew vegetables. People with gardens were encouraged to grow their own food: *"You grew as many vegetables as you could."* At Ness Gardens Josiah Hope, the head gardener, used the little labour he still had to concentrate on vegetables and fruit — mainly gooseberries, apples and pears. These were sold to Mr Peters, a Neston greengrocer.

The Crossleys had a market garden at Willaston where, before the war, they had grown vegetables and chrysanthemums. Under the War Ag's direction they were no longer allowed to grow flowers, and grew lettuces instead. They got a greenhouse and a coke ration to prepare early crops. As well as lettuce, they grew early broad beans under glass, and outside grew cabbages, cauliflowers, potatoes and radishes. They had to be seen to be distributing their produce to shops at controlled prices, and their trading records were checked.

Like most farming activities before modern mechanical methods were introduced in the second half of the twentieth century, fruit picking was a labour-intensive task. In 1940, these Neston Rangers were gathering plums in Ledbury, Herefordshire.

Another smallholder was George McMaster, who foresaw that food would be scarce in wartime and decided to learn farming from scratch. Knowing nothing about agriculture, he went to Sussex to learn, and then bought sixteen acres off The Runnel. There he and his family grew potatoes and had two large greenhouses for tomatoes and other crops. Eventually they had sixteen cows, 3,000 chickens and some turkeys. But Mr McMaster died during the war, and friends and neighbours, including the Crossleys, rallied round with help and advice so that his daughter could continue.

With so many men joining the armed forces, labour was a problem for farmers. George Langley, who had an anti-aircraft battery nearby, was able to employ two or three soldiers when he needed them. He had the agonizing task of having to decide which of two brothers who worked for him, Ernie and Henry Rimmel, should go into the armed forces and which should be granted a reserved occupation and stay on the farm. Langley went to the War Ag office in Chester in August 1941 to discuss Ernie, the one who had to go. He also employed Tom Jones, a conscientious objector who was posted to the farm. Another source of labour was the Land Girls. The Women's Land Army was formed in July 1939, but it was an army in name only, with no discipline, although they did have a uniform. Girls were billeted in private houses, and Mrs Millington had two with her in Neston. *"They were an asset, bringing eggs, cuts of bacon and bantam hens to supplement the rations."* There do not seem to have been many of them locally: Karl Jennings employed some in his market garden department in 1942, but when George Langley wanted one in 1944, he *"went to Chester to try to get a Land Girl, but no luck"*. He succeeded in getting one shortly afterwards and another one later. They travelled by bicycle from Bebington and Birkenhead. In 1943 Italian prisoners of war became available for farm work, and German prisoners became available when a camp opened at Ledsham in late 1944.

The local fishermen were operating in sensitive waters as Liverpool became the chief entry point for imports to Britain.

> *The fishermen who hadn't been called up were given a sketch map of Liverpool Bay showing areas of water which had been filled with mines — these were prohibited areas for us to fish. We were also issued with sets of signal flags of different colours to fly on specified days of the week, to show the Examination Vessel at the mouth of the Dee that we were genuine fishermen. The trouble was that most people got fed up trying to remember which flag was for which day and just used them as rags to polish the engine, so they gradually became*

a mucky grey colour. Good job the crew of the Examination Vessel got to know us — we used to pass them a bucket of fresh fish whenever we saw them — as none of us ever remembered the password for the day, which we were also supposed to give.

These were dangerous waters, and several local men, including Chris Peters, saw a coasting vessel, the *Maurita*, blow up when it hit a mine at the mouth of the estuary. Fortunately for the Parkgate fishermen, many of the large trawlers from Fleetwood and other ports had been requisitioned as minesweepers, being built of wood. Therefore the fish were breeding abundantly as fewer were caught.

Some of the fishermen who were left made small fortunes during the war, as there was such a shortage of food that there was never any trouble selling the catch. We sent sacks of cockles and mussels to market by rail from Parkgate station every day, and a regular lorry would come out from the dealers in Liverpool to collect the fish for the fish market. We had a ready market for our shrimps, which we sold straight to the Grosvenor Hotel in Chester or Reece's Restaurant in Liverpool.

Some of their neighbours took fish in their briefcases on the bus to sell at work in Liverpool.

It is indeed an ill wind that blows nobody any good. In the Queen's Channel in Liverpool Bay there was an area of 'spoiled ground' where ships had been mined and sunk. Around these wrecks there was an abundance of small sole to be caught. Meanwhile, times were changing at Parkgate. It was during the war that the channel became so shallow that the fishing boats were moored at Thurstaston or Heswall, and the catch was sometimes put on the train at Thurstaston station, the men returning to Parkgate by rowing boat or punt.

As well as the Dig for Victory campaign, there was also official encouragement to keep hens, rabbits and pigs to supplement the meat ration. In August 1940 Neston Council informed its tenants that any restriction on keeping such animals was suspended during the war.

The elegant Lady Marcia Miles came to school to give us a talk on the finer points of rabbit breeding. She left us with a supply of very informative leaflets and the suggestion of forming a school rabbit club, which would entitle members to a bran ration for feeding them. I already had a little Dutch doe which Andrew Prince had given me, and Mr Exton [the headmaster] appointed me rabbit club secretary, responsible for doling out the bran ration and doing the paperwork.

Chapter Seven

But Colin Foote discovered a snag. Although he had no qualms about 'necking' a wild rabbit caught in a snare or in a net when pursued by his ferret, he could not bring himself to kill his captive rabbits. He also kept bantams which fostered day-old chicks bought from Bibby's at Willaston for a penny each.

In Parkgate Emily Anderson and her daughter Jean kept rabbits in a shed and a long fenced run. They sold the meat and Mrs Anderson cured the skins herself and sold them to furriers to make gloves, hats or coats.

One method of supplementing the rations was to find friends in Wales:

> *As food was scarce, Gran sometimes took two of my aunts with her on a long trip to visit her friends who farmed beyond Mold. It was worth the three bus journeys and a walk to get there. They would come back late, laden with joints of salted ham and bacon, all home cured, jars of honey, cheese, butter and eggs, to dish out to the rest of the family.*

Mostyn House also made much use of its Welsh connection, and the school's farm at Cerrigydrudion helped to eke out the rations. Erma Grenfell, wife of the headmaster, used to tour the surrounding villages to buy large quantities of fruit, which she bottled. She made jam and butter, preserved eggs in isinglass, and cured ham.

Neston was still a rural village in the 1940s, and many of its people were accustomed to being 'hunter-gatherers'. The marsh helped to support those who went wildfowling as it had always supported the fishermen: *"We lived off the marsh in the winter months when there was no fishing, and shot for food, not just for the sport."* There were certain wild birds' eggs which made welcome eating in the spring: waterhens', plovers' and gulls'. Boys would take alternate new-laid eggs from the nests of coots or waterhens, marking the others in soft pencil and then leaving the birds to sit in peace when the clutch was complete. For the amateur fishermen there were flounders and eels, shrimps and cockles, and *"Every marl pit held fish, muddy flavoured unless well fried."* Gleaning came back into fashion as farmers let people search their fields, after the harvest, for grain to feed poultry. Mushrooms, blackberries, crab-apples, sweet chestnuts and hazelnuts were all gathered in their season. The Grenfells' three daughters learned to shoot rabbits and to use a ferret.

It was not just food that was gathered. Coal was rationed, and when the supply ran short, people would scavenge for pieces of coal on the colliery waste tip at the bottom of Marshlands Road.

Mrs Crook's main memory was of making meals out of nothing, such as cake without eggs, though powdered egg was quite good. Her family ate a lot of potatoes, as they were plentiful and would keep. She took scraps to a woman who had chickens and she would get a couple of eggs in return. Bill Jones's gran made her butter ration go further by mixing it with margarine, eggs, baking powder and milk: *"It was quite acceptable if she got the ingredients right."* But there were frustrations, including queuing. And for once, the shopkeeper had the upper hand. Before the war, "almost all provisions were delivered and local tradespeople waited on us hand and foot for a few shillings' worth of orders." But now it was the housewife who waited, queued and hoped.

> *The thing that stands out in my mind* [wrote Bill Jones] *is that ours was a large family, that spent a lot of money at our shop, yet when the sweets came in (which we found out by bush telegraph) we would be served with inferior stuff like liquorice allsorts, while people who had big houses and plenty of money but small purchases would be given the best of the consignment, like chocolate and caramel. There were other shops where people were treated with arrogance, simply because they could not leave and shop elsewhere.*

Of course most shopkeepers were doing their best: "We were short of many things in the shop. There was a great shortage of writing paper as wives wanted to write to husbands away."

The matron at Mostyn House told Mr Grenfell that there was a serious crisis: she had run out of lavatory paper. He drove round the villages of North Wales, buying every roll of toilet paper he could find.

The black market was much talked about during the war, but was little in evidence for most people. The black market meant illegal trading in rationed goods. One local grocer was reported to the food office for selling rationed goods without first taking the coupons from the ration book. Certain Neston tradespeople were said to gather in the Shrewsbury Arms on Sunday evenings to arrange shady deals. Geoff Nicholls thought that such deals usually consisted of smuggling the odd pig past the food control. He himself found that one of his pigs had died from a heart attack, and, while it was still warm, he surreptitiously took it in his car to a local butcher. According to Graham Langley it was reputed that a farm in Neston had a hollow haystack where pigs and sheep were slaughtered illicitly. The Parkgate fishermen *"were allowed extra petrol coupons for the boat's engine. Some people did a lucrative deal with one of the local garages and friends to supply them with unwanted but precious petrol coupons."*

Eating out was still possible, although hotels and restaurants were not allowed to charge more than five shillings for a meal. Hylda Wall-Jones was taken to lunch one day by her brother to the Union Hotel in Parkgate. It was a ghastly meal and her brother thundered, *"I would like to see the manager. Please bring him." "I am sorry, sir,"* muttered the waiter, *"he has gone out for lunch."*

In some places, though not in the Neston area, the Government ran 'British Restaurants', which were like canteens open to the public. There was one at Little Sutton which Bill Jones remembered with pleasure:

Anybody could walk in and purchase a dinner and sweet, which would be mince, carrots, potatoes and gravy, with a cake-type pudding and runny custard, all I think for one shilling. To a lad who had been delivering bread all day and with a stomach that thought my throat had been cut, this was the ultimate in cuisine, runny custard or no.

The rations situation for families was eased, at least in term time, by the introduction of school meals in 1943: *"March 28th, 'provision of dinners' scheme commenced in this school* [Liverpool Road] *at a charge of two shillings per child each week."*

The women's organizations were of course in the forefront of the battle to provide food. Had the need arisen, the Neston WVS would have manned an emergency feeding station for up to 120 refugees at Harry Prosser's Deeside Café in Parkgate. The local Women's Institutes at Willaston and Burton & Puddington had lectures on wartime cookery and fruit bottling. The Ministry of Food provided sugar to the WIs, who ran co-operative jam-making depots and made huge quantities of jam, marmalade, chutney and pickles. The produce had to be checked by an inspector, who rejected very few jars and marked most boilings as *"excellent"*. The WIs had to pay for the hire of premises, equipment, including boilers and a canning machine, the cost of the sugar and of fruit at wholesale prices, except for blackberries which were picked by members. Most of the produce was sold locally, with some going to Leasowe Hospital for Children and some to shops. A retail licence had to be obtained from Neston Food Office, and permits for soap, tea and sugar for the distribution centre. The profits were used to buy more equipment, or invested in war savings, or were given to other war efforts.

WI members were encouraged to grow vegetables, and leaflets were provided by the War Ag at Reaseheath with advice. They received seeds and fertilizer from Canada. At Willaston they held a competition for the most potatoes grown from a single tuber, the resulting crop being given

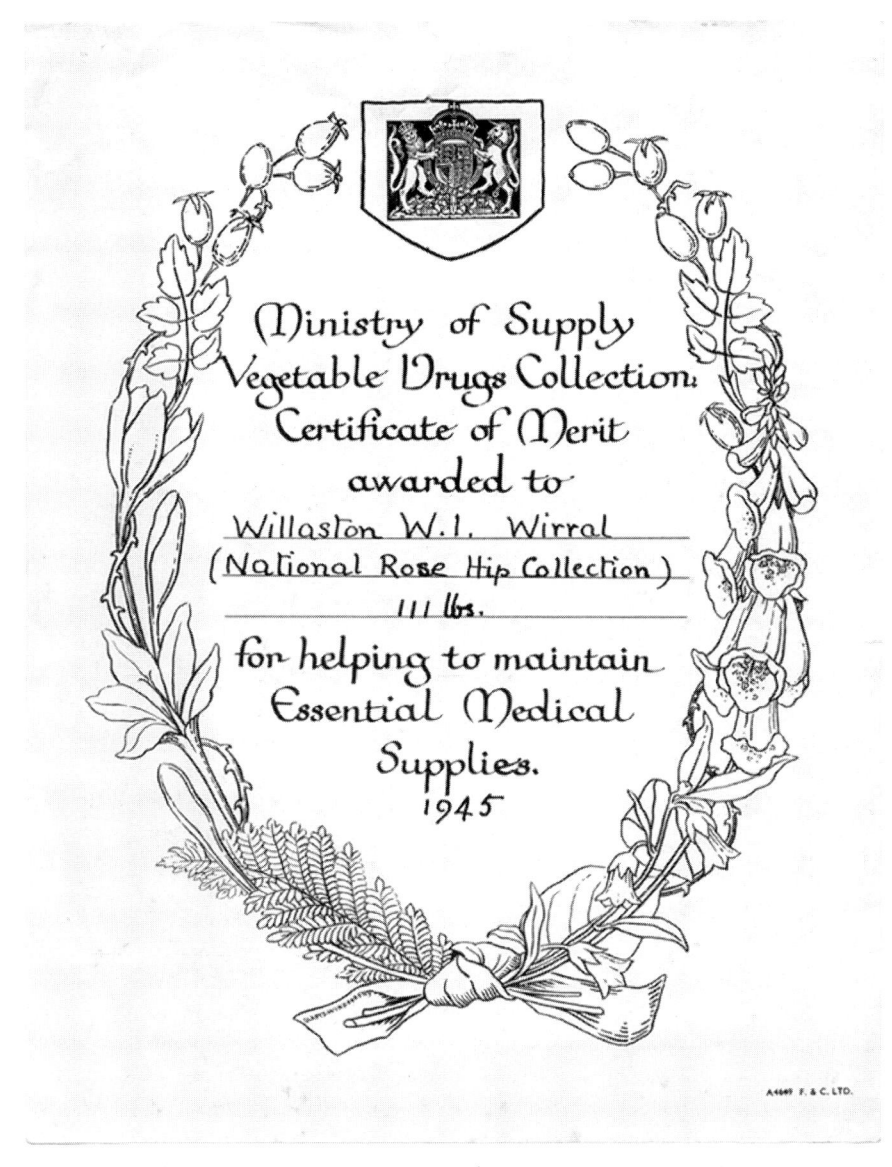

> Ministry of Supply
> Vegetable Drugs Collection.
> Certificate of Merit
> awarded to
> Willaston W.I. Wirral
> (National Rose Hip Collection)
> 111 lbs.
> for helping to maintain
> Essential Medical
> Supplies.
> 1945

Local Women's Institutes played their part in collecting flowers, fruits and plants from the hedgerow and garden. Rosehips were a valuable source of Vitamin C.

in 1940 to the Neston cottage hospital. Vegetables were sometimes collected for such recipients as the Willaston searchlight battery or minesweeper crews. The WIs also distributed orange juice and cod liver oil for babies in their villages, after overcoming some resistance from Neston Food Office, which expected everybody to come to them.

Members also collected wild plants. For medical purposes, coltsfoot, foxgloves and raspberry leaves were gathered, while dried herbs, including thyme, mint, sage, marjoram and parsley, were sent to the Red Cross for prisoner-of-war parcels. Nettles were collected in large quantities and dried for the extraction of chlorophyll to be used as a dye. Willaston was also asked to dry dark peony petals, the source of peonidin, a red dye. Rosehips, which provided essential Vitamin C for babies, were collected in large quantities. The Ministry of Supply, unable to import enough oranges, would pay 2d. a pound for them. *"They are about twenty times richer in Vitamin C than oranges, and they can be made into a syrup which babies love and take readily."* As well as the WIs and schools, Miss Barber's Girl Guides gathered rosehips. In Neston they were taken to Miss Blain at the WVS office, or to Mr Helm at Willaston school. They were then sent to a wholesale chemist in Liverpool.

There was a shortage of meat, not only because it could not be imported, but because the considerable quantities of feedstuffs needed for our own

Children volunteered, or were pressed into service, too. Here, Miss Blain of the WVS, Barbara Davies, Norma and Max Grant, and Joe Downey pick rosehips on Burton Common in 1943.

cattle could no longer be imported. The domestic meat ration was very small, and the Ministry of Food wished to boost the supply for workers, many of whom could get cheap meals from factory canteens or British Restaurants. To extend this provision to rural and agricultural workers, the WVS publicized the 'Rural District Pie Scheme' in mid-1942. It was not until May 1943, however, following an uncooperative response from the Neston Food Control Committee, which considered the scheme unnecessary, and bewildering bureaucratic demands, that the WIs, responsible for organizing the scheme in this area, were able to start. They had to arrange to have the pies made by a baker. These were then sold for 4d. for a small pie or pasty, and 1s. 4d. for a large pie. Customers had to order them, and in Willaston the pies were distributed twice a week from the Institute or the adjacent War Memorial Hut. By the end of the war, Willaston alone had sold 128,000, and a further 62,000 were sold before the scheme ended in 1949. The accumulated profits were eventually, in 1980, used to buy tables for Willaston Memorial Hall.

Chapter Seven

SOURCES

This chapter was written by Geoffrey Place.

Details of the allotments were provided by Susan Chambers, and Hilary Morris used the records of the Willaston and Burton & Puddington Women's Institutes for her account of their activities.

We are grateful to Mary Chrimes for her description of the food office; to Reg Bushell, Kath Bushell, Derek Mellor and Chris Peters for their record of fishing; to Karl Jennings, Graham Langley and Geoff Nicholls for their memories of farming; to Colin Foote for his record of food gathering; to Julian Grenfell for access to the Mostyn House archives; and to Joyce Barber, Marie Crook, Lettice Crossley, Anne Gray, Miss Hope, Bill Jones, Kathleen Kinnaston (née Gray), Jane Macdonald, Anne Millington, Bill Pye, Mrs Reece, Molly Roberts and Hylda Wall-Jones.

CHAPTER EIGHT

THE HOME FRONT: WORKING FOR THE WAR EFFORT

We boys would have followed Churchill to hell and back, and we hung on his every word. We knew, for he said so, that the Home Front was equally as important as those far-off battle campaigns.

Churchill became Prime Minister on 10 May 1940, after Chamberlain, who had brought us into the war with many misgivings, had resigned. He was old and ill, and died five months later. Churchill had consistently warned of the danger of Hitler and the Nazis, and was generally welcomed, but the same day that he assumed office, Germany invaded Belgium, Holland and France, and the British Army was forced to retreat from the beaches of Dunkirk. Yet Churchill's obstinate determination, his realism (*"I have nothing to offer but blood, toil, tears and sweat"*) and his growling voice combined to unite the country into wholehearted support for the struggle against Germany. This surprised Hitler, who had thought that Britain would make peace.

The phrase *"Don't you know there's a war on?"* was used to explain or excuse every shortage and irritation which war conditions imposed on everybody. And there were many. As well as the food shortage which has been described, clothes were in short supply, and from June 1941 could be bought only with one's ration of coupons:

> *You couldn't buy new clothes, so most people made do with hand-me-downs or managed to buy material to make things. Sometimes they could use unwanted blackout curtains or even white parachute silk if they could get any. Discarded army coats were prized as they were very thick and warm for going on the marsh.*

From 1942 'utility' clothes were available, made in as few styles and with as little material as possible.

Transport was another problem. Petrol was rationed at the start of the war, and in 1942 the civilian ration was cut off. Charles Gray, who ran a threshing machine and timber business from the mill in Leighton Road, was a group organizer of petrol rationing for commercial vehicles. People with vans and lorries came to his house on Friday nights to collect their coupons. There was a speed limit of 20 m.p.h. in built-up areas and the blackout imposed its own limits. Most private cars were 'laid-up' by placing brick pillars under the axles to preserve the tyres; and in October 1942 the *Liverpool Daily Post* reported a census ordered by the Government of all laid-up cars in case they or their tyres were needed. Public transport was frequently disrupted, because of military priorities, shortages or bombing, although war work meant that more people were on the move than ever. The Crosville bus company advertised in the local papers to urge people not to travel unnecessarily at rush hours as the buses were overcrowded. In 1942 Neston Council asked Burton Road school to alter its opening time to stagger the use of buses. In the same year, queue lines were painted at Neston Cross to ease the pressure when buses were boarded, but the markings were not found satisfactory, partly because people could not see them in the blackout, and queue barriers were requested.

The difficulties of travelling are illustrated by Arnold Whiteway's experience when he came home on leave from the Royal Navy. He caught the last ferry at half-past midnight (the ferry captains were adept at crossing in the dark without lights) and slept on a bench at Woodside to await the 6.30 a.m. bus. But bombs began to fall, so he walked to Clatterbridge, where he hoped to hitch a lift in the early mail van out of Birkenhead. The porter at Clatterbridge hospital gave him tea and toasted buns to warm him up; but the mail van did not arrive and Arnold walked the rest of the way to Neston.

Almost the whole of the civilian population was actively engaged in the war effort. All men between the ages of 18 and 40 were liable for conscription into the armed forces. A Register of Employment was started for both men and women, and men under 60 could be directed to serve part-time in Civil Defence or the Home Guard. Unmarried women aged between 20 and 30 were also conscripted, but could choose the auxiliary services (WRNS, ATS, WAAF) or industry. Ernest Bevin, the Minister of Labour, had far-reaching powers at his disposal, but he chose to use them sparingly. In December 1941 the Ministry of Labour & National Service wrote to Daryl Grenfell to enquire about the nature of Miss M. Pearson's employment at Mostyn House, as *"young, mobile women should be released for the women's services and for industry"*. But Marjorie Pearson remained on the domestic staff throughout the war. When Marie Crook went to the employment office she was pregnant. When she told the man that the baby was due, *"he could not get me out of the office quickly enough."*

Under the Essential Work Order of 1941, workers in some jobs could not leave their employment, or be dismissed from it. But work in the war factories was very popular because the wages were good. Ruth Roberts was in service before the war, being paid 15 shillings a week as *"there was no other work around except the laundry and mother would not let us go there."* When she was twenty she was called up, and for four years worked in the Vickers-Armstrong aircraft factory at Broughton, near Hawarden, which built Wellington bombers and, from 1943, Lancasters. It was a totally new experience for her:

> *We were not used to crowds of people or the buses. The first day we took our time and did not rush and all the buses had gone. We knew next day to clock off and go. I got £7 a week and was thrilled to bits. We got production money if the output was over a certain amount.*

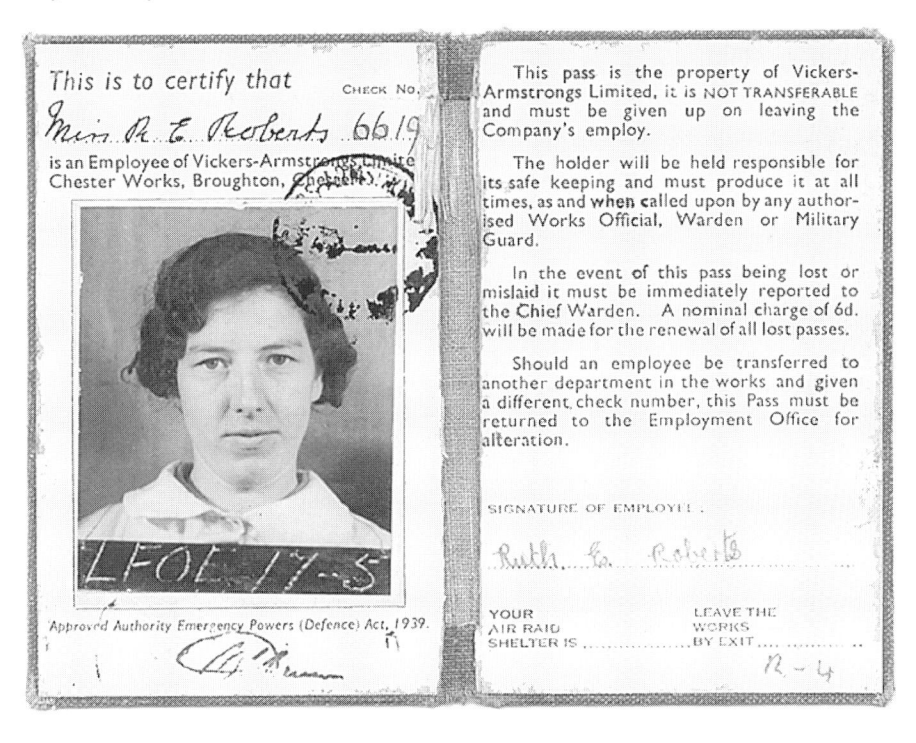

Strict security was an important matter in places of work where sabotage would have harmed the national capacity to carry the fight to the enemy.

Chapter Eight

But the need for aircraft was so vital that, driven by Lord Beaverbrook, the Minister for Aircraft Production, the hours were very long. Ruth worked a twelve-hour shift, six days a week, and eventually worked a night shift, with a fortnight on nights and a fortnight on day shift. Her bus left Neston at 7 a.m. and she returned home at 9 p.m., so she had no time to spend her money.

> *When I first started I was on the petrol system, fixing fuel pipes. I didn't like it. The group of men didn't like women there, so I was transferred to a joiner's job.*

She fitted wooden strips to the metal fuselage of the plane to hold down the canvas cover, which was then painted with dope.

> *We were compelled to wear trousers and overalls because of the climbing and lying under the plane.*

One day a bomber was completed in 24 hours. She was so tired that when she left she walked into a camouflage pole and bruised her face.

HRH the Duke of Kent visits the Vickers-Armstrong aircraft factory at Broughton. The basket-like geodetic aluminium frames of Wellington bombers can be seen under construction.

There were two Royal Ordnance factories run by the Ministry of Supply in which Neston people worked — at Hooton and at Capenhurst. In the

The Home Front: Working for the War Effort

country as a whole, there had been three Royal Ordnance factories in 1936 when British rearmament started; fourteen were in operation by mid-1940 and 44 by 1945. The Hooton factory was known as Roften, or Royal Ordnance Factory No.10. It was an engineering works making gun barrels. Later, jerry cans to hold petrol or water were made there. The Ministry of Supply built houses, with flat roofs to avoid the use of scarce timber, in Willaston largely for the managers, many of whom were seconded from the Royal Ordnance factory at Woolwich, and other workers were housed at Little Sutton in similar houses. A Neston lad called Henry Fleming worked there and lost his life when his head was crushed in a machine. After the war the factory was occupied by Williams & Williams of Chester, who made prefabricated houses.

The Capenhurst works was not a factory, but a 'small arms ammunition inspection centre'. Anne Gray worked there for five years. Her job was to inspect bullets of three types: for .303 rifles, for Sten guns and for medium machine-guns, which had been manufactured at Woolwich Arsenal. Each bullet was checked to ensure perfection, with every scratch rubbed away, and then checked a second time by someone else. The girls had to wear headscarves to avoid dust, and to ensure concentration they were not allowed to talk, although they could sing. The bullets were then packed into cases for despatch overseas, usually through Liverpool. Miss Gray also used to pack uniforms in hessian, pieces of which she put inside her shoes to keep warm. She used to travel to Capenhurst by train, leaving home at 6.30 a.m. to start work at 7.30, work till 5.30 p.m. and get home an hour later. The trains were unreliable and sometimes she had to wait for hours at Hooton station or walk from there. Ruth Roberts transferred from Broughton to Capenhurst towards the end of the war and travelled there by bicycle.

As well as the large factories, there were many small engineering works engaged in war work, mostly set up in garages which had lost their motor trade. One of these was Frank Kyffin's Five Ways garage on the Chester High Road. Roy Booth worked there while too young to be called up, and was surprised to find that girls were doing both electric and gas welding. They were making parts for Bailey bridges and aerial torpedo cases. In the electric welding shop there were fourteen girls and seven men; in the gas welding shop there were ten girls. Emily Oxton worked as an electric welder, and remembers being burned by the sparks, despite her leather apron. The men wore helmets with shields to protect their eyes, but the girls preferred hand-held visors, which did not mess up their hair. *"We were all locals and knew each other, so it was a happy place."* After the war, Frank Kyffin made parts for prefabricated houses.

Victor Horsman, who had a motorcycle engineering works in Liverpool, relocated in Neston at Fleming's yard in Leighton Road. Mary Sir worked there making aeroplane parts which were so secret that the workforce of about thirty people, mainly men bussed in from Liverpool, did not know what they were for. Reg Leeman's garage on the Parkgate Parade was similarly engaged in war work: Tommy Maddox worked there for four years from the age of 14, using brass and aluminium to make parts for aircraft engines and also for tanks. He remembers an army officer coming to test the penetrative qualities of a plastic, which he did by firing at it with his revolver.

There were many other such small workshops in the area. Lloyd's garage in Willaston made shell cases. The Wheatsheaf garage at Mollington assembled army vehicles. One Parkgate resident was sent to work at Blake's garage in City Road, Chester. It had been taken over by Rootes, who made parts for Lancaster bombers. When she first went she *"didn't know a nut from a bolt"*, but she learned to operate a drill to make aeroplane parts. Although the hours were long, *"Everyone was so nice and kind: they were pleasant and worked as a team."* She rose at 6 a.m., reaching Chester by cycle and train to start work at 8 o'clock, and sometimes did not finish until 9 p.m.

Mr J. R. Davies, the headmaster of Ness Holt school.

It was not just the adults who were fully involved in the war effort, for the children felt that they were too. Bill Jones was at Ness Holt school:

The headmaster, Mr J. R. Davies, was an ex-First-World-War soldier who made sure we never forgot that Britain was at war with a deadly enemy. He organized egg weeks, when we brought in an egg from our rations. This resulted in hundreds of eggs being sent away to help the war effort. He had us all collecting scrap iron, and we certainly had the playground full to capacity; we even collected German shrapnel to add to the tonnage. Then he had us collecting rosehips for medical syrup and also nettles, which I can only assume were again for medical use. But before they were sent away they were hung up in the classroom to dry out. What a palaver that was, trying to read or write with green caterpillars dropping on your books or down your neck. But he still wasn't done with us. Our next task was knitting squares for blankets for the services, boys as well as girls. It was only a plain stitch but we certainly turned out a few blankets, balaclavas and gloves.

The headmaster at Burton Road, A. J. Exton, was just as fiercely patriotic:

The walls of the central school assembly hall were well papered with posters saying 'Careless Talk Costs Lives' and 'Dig for Victory'. Mr Exton had rousing marching music played on the piano at lesson-changing time, and we all had to march between classrooms to improve school efficiency.

Both schools took digging for victory very seriously. At Ness Holt they cultivated half an acre behind the Wheatsheaf, led by class leaders. The resulting vegetables were sold cheaply to pupils' parents. The profits were used to buy a radio and speakers to each classroom. Some children could become more directly involved in agriculture:

About 1943 any pupil aged 13 or more could go and work on the farms at harvest time, as labour was scarce and more land was being planted with corn and potatoes. You were given a card with fourteen half-day sections. Every half-day worked had to be signed by the farmer to prove you were not playing truant. This was a godsend for my pals and me, as we used it right up to the last half-day, and we went harvesting when we knew there were lessons we did not like.

Mr A. J. Exton, the headmaster of Burton Road school.

At Burton Road, Mr Exton was a keen gardener and a perfectionist, directing 'learning on the job' garden training for senior boys while girls were doing domestic science. If an urgent task was required in the garden, Mr Exton would burst into a classroom and divert a couple of lads from their classwork to get it done. One such lad was Tom Johnson. "Johnson, go and tidy those cauliflowers." "Cauliflowers, sir?" "Yes, yes, tidy up the leaves." "Yes, sir", said Tom, and set about the task he thought was required. When Mr Exton saw the resulting row of little white flower heads and no leaves at all, he was not amused.

Neston lads, probably like those everywhere else, had a mania for collecting war souvenirs. This was despite an official warning: *"The public are specially warned against collecting souvenirs. They may be dangerous and may be wanted by the authorities for investigation."*

In Willaston the older boys used to clear the anti-aircraft shell shrapnel from the church roof, and David Woodhouse could walk to school in the morning and see shrapnel everywhere. The boys would compete to find the largest pieces. In Parkgate this kind of collecting could take a more serious turn. The boys were constantly trying to sneak into military camps like the searchlight battery or the former Leighton School in Boathouse Lane:

> *We would get some of the girls to go and talk to the sentry on duty while we sneaked in to see what we could find. Once one of the boys, Snob Jones, found a new grenade in the stores, but as he went to throw it, it exploded and he lost his eye. We all got a severe telling-off in school about this, but the fascination was too much for us and we were soon back again pestering the soldiers. We used to collect spent rounds of ammunition, and once we found some live .303 bullets. Someone lit a bonfire and threw handfuls on the fire to watch them explode! We could all have been killed. We also collected brass shells, fins from cylinders, all sorts of useless fascinating bits and pieces.*

This type of lawlessness was seen as a symptom of the absence of so many fathers and the upheaval caused by war conditions. In April 1941 there was an outbreak of apparently wilful smashing of windows and milk bottles. A year later the council was writing to the Chief Constable to ask for stricter policing after an outbreak of hooliganism throughout the district, including damage to property in Ness. Strict blackout was ended in September 1944, followed by a 'dim-out' until the end of the war. The reappearance of street lights was too much for some, and damage to them was reported in February 1945.

Some boys, such as the Neston Sea Scouts, were more usefully employed:

> *We had been taught how to deal with incendiary bombs, using stirrup pumps. We formed teams to erect the Morrison table shelters for old people and young wives whose husbands were on active service. Older lads put in a rota as ARP messengers and fire-watchers.*

ARP messengers were supposed to be 14 or more, but Ken Johnson was appointed a runner for the Home Guard when only about nine years old.

The Home Front: Working for the War Effort

MINISTRY OF SUPPLY

EVERY SCRAP AND EVERY KIND OF RAG IS NEEDED NOW!

Rags are needed so urgently that the Government have had to make an Order that rags must not be destroyed, thrown away or mixed with refuse. They make so many vital articles of Service equipment. Every woman should start a rag bag; and put in it every scrap of unwanted rag that can be turned out of cupboard, drawer and work-basket.

START A RAG BAG

PUT IN YOUR RAG BAG all those bits and pieces of wool, cotton, silk and linen you've been saving up but will never really use: dress-making snippets and clippings: ends of sewing cotton and knitting wool: old clothing, towels and dusters past repair: bits of sacking and canvas: old clothes-line, cord, string. *Dirty, oily and paint-stained rags are as valuable as clean ones, but should be kept separate.*

PUT YOUR RAGS OUT with your other salvage, in a separate dry bundle ready for collection by the Local Authority. Or sell them to the Rag and Bone Man.

WHEN YOUR RAG BAG IS EMPTIED FILL IT UP AGAIN! Rags make blankets, battle-dress, greatcoats; haversacks, webbing equipment; paper, maps, charts; wipers for aero-engines; surgical equipment ... and thousands of other vitally essential munitions of war.

People were exhorted to collect for recycling many items of waste which would normally have been thrown away. As this notice shows, it was illegal to discard some materials.

Chapter Eight

He practised taking messages from the lookout on the colliery site to the police station, following the Stanney brook by crawling through the culvert under Bridge Street.

At Thornton Hough school, the older children had to join a Young Farmers' Club, the nearest being in Willaston, or the Army, Air Force or Sea Cadets.

It was not only the schoolchildren who collected scrap metal. Everybody was constantly urged to save any materials which could be recycled. 'Salvage' was the order of the day, and a cartoon character called the Squanderbug was used to exhort people to waste nothing. Scraps of food were to be set aside to feed pigs, and bins were placed in the streets to receive them. There were white-painted bins for bones, but these were abandoned because of dog nuisance. There were collections of textiles, rubber, boots and shoes, bottles and jam jars, often assisted by children, including the Scouts and Guides. As well as rosehips, they also gathered acorns and conkers for pig food. In April 1944 thirty thousand books were collected, to restock bombed libraries, for recycling and to send to the troops. As the *Liverpool Echo* put it,

Books for the airmen who fly in the sky,
Books for the soldiers who fight till they die...

A popular item for collection, though officially frowned on, was the silk from parachute flares.

In 1942 the council required Neston's refuse collectors, in addition to their usual work, to collect paper, metal and bones. They were supposed to keep these materials separate in their lorry, but those householders who had conscientiously sorted them were not pleased to see them thrown together with the rubbish. A shed was provided at the tip to hold bottles and metal objects. Some of the salvage was stored in the basement of the town hall, resulting in trouble with rats.

Salvage on a large scale was evident in Neston at the timber dumps. These were part of a national scheme to save used timber from bombed buildings and ships which had been stripped of their peacetime fittings. By the end of 1941, hundreds of former passenger ships and coasters had been requisitioned as troop and supply carriers, and many tons of timber from cabins, decks and other furnishings were being heaped around the docks at Birkenhead and Liverpool. There it was a fire risk, so the timber was brought out to Neston. Some of the timber was of very high quality: large sections of mahogany from luxury passenger cabins, teak decking, wooden masts, bird's-eye maple used for dance floors, ships' staircases and baulks of beautiful yellow pine. There were also huge crates which had contained aeroplane parts shipped as deck cargo from the United States, and a large consignment of damaged timber from bombed-out homes in Liverpool and Birkenhead — roof spars and purlins, windows and doors.

Thomas Norman of Little Neston, a builder, was paid by Neston Council to organize a suitable site, and the first dump was started on a narrow strip between Burton Road and the railway. A second site was found in a field on the way to Ness, employing women from the colliery area. The largest site was the field beside Badger Bait, then a narrow winding lane, where the Rose Gardens houses were later built. Jim Bushell, who had lost a lung and so could not enlist, was in charge.

Until the removal of iron railings, supposedly to help the war effort, was made compulsory in 1941, the parish church of St Mary and St Helen in Neston possessed fine railings and gates.

The aircraft crates, twenty feet long, made garden sheds, while masts made gateposts. When the timber arrived it was sorted into stacks by length and type of wood. Better quality wood was made into furniture. Much of the wood was used on local farms for fencing, chicken sheds, shippons and farm buildings. A five-ton lorry load cost £5 and the supply

Chapter Eight

was plentiful. The dumps also sold nails and screws pulled out of the wood and sorted into drums for the scrap man. Strips of phosphor bronze were also sold for threshold pieces or stair treads.

A less successful local operation was the collection of tin cans. Large numbers were collected, but they then had to be flattened. A steam roller was tried, but with no success, so a baling press was borrowed from the Royal Engineers. The result was 350 cubic yards of tins that nobody actually wanted. Eventually they were buried at the tip at Tanks Field.

There were constant exhortations from the Government to keep the drive for salvage going, and in early 1942 a County Salvage Drive was organized. Loudspeaker vans provided by the Ministry of Information toured Neston, and public meetings were held. A hundred salvage stewards were enrolled through the WVS, and sacks were distributed for street paper collections.

"Raw material is war material" was the slogan on advertisements to save paper. In early 1940 Neston Council asked householders to keep papers, magazines and cardboard separate from their household rubbish. The dustmen collected it and the council bought a paper-baling machine (*"one man, a boy or even a woman can operate it"*). The baled paper was sold, five tons at a time, to a mill in Warrington, at £3 a ton, increased to £6 as the shortage of paper became more severe. Neston continued to collect and sell its waste paper until 1970.

One of the best-remembered forms of salvage was the collection of iron railings. At first the surrender of railings was voluntary, and among those taken were the railings that divided the boys' and girls' playgrounds at Burton Road school, railings round graves in the churchyard that had blown down the previous winter, those in front of all 31 houses in Gladstone Road, and the cemetery railings. But in September 1941 the council was required to make

It is thought that William and Mary, two eighteenth-century mooring anchors, were not saved by their antiquity when scrap metal was collected by the authorities.

The Home Front: Working for the War Effort

a survey of all unnecessary railings in the district, and any which deserved to be kept because of artistic or historic interest had to be registered with the Town Clerk. Under this provision the gates of Stanney Park were removed and stored. Some people kept their gates by burying them in the garden. Those railings that were requisitioned were removed by the Ministry of Works in December 1942. It was not only railings that went: at Mostyn House there was a large German mortar, presented to the school after the First World War, and appropriately enough it went to help fight the Germans. Less happily, two large mooring anchors, used at the Parkgate anchorage in the early eighteenth century and latterly stored at Mostyn House, were also taken for scrap. Much of the scrap metal collected in Neston was not used, and rusted away on a dump at Greasby.

Andrew Prince tells the story of Dr Yeoman, when the men came to take the railings from the front of his house, Elmhurst, in Parkgate Road. He told them that his railings were made of wood, and to prove it he cut a piece from one of them with his penknife and the men went away. In fact only one railing was wooden, made by his gardener to replace a broken metal one.

Mr G. H. Fowles, headmaster of Liverpool Road school.

If salvage became a wartime obsession, so did National Savings. It started in the schools, where G. H. Fowles, headmaster of Liverpool Road school, was secretary of the National Savings Movement. And *"We must save till it hurts"* was Mr Exton's almost daily call to his pupils at Burton Road:

Charismatic and more Churchillian in some ways than the great man himself, Mr Exton ran a tight ship. We all had National Savings books, and teachers had to mark up the 3d. or 6d. contributions and balance the books.

For adults, there were annual calls to give money for the war effort: the Spitfire Fund in 1940 for which the Junkers 88 was displayed at Parkgate (£13 million was raised nationally), War Weapons Week in 1941, Warship Week in 1942, Wings for Victory in 1943, Salute the Soldier in 1944. Some

Chapter Eight

THIS
CERTIFICATE OF HONOUR
IS AWARDED TO

Willaston 15A/1/13

SAVINGS GROUP

IN RECOGNITION OF SPECIAL ACHIEVEMENT
DURING THE

WINGS FOR VICTORY
NATIONAL SAVINGS CAMPAIGN 1943

I EXTEND MY THANKS TO ALL CONCERNED
IN THIS IMPORTANT NATIONAL SERVICE.

Archibald Sinclair
SECRETARY OF STATE FOR AIR

Above and facing page: The National Savings movement held special fund-raising campaigns for the armed services, which focused on a different beneficiary each year. Local effort was rewarded with a certificate.

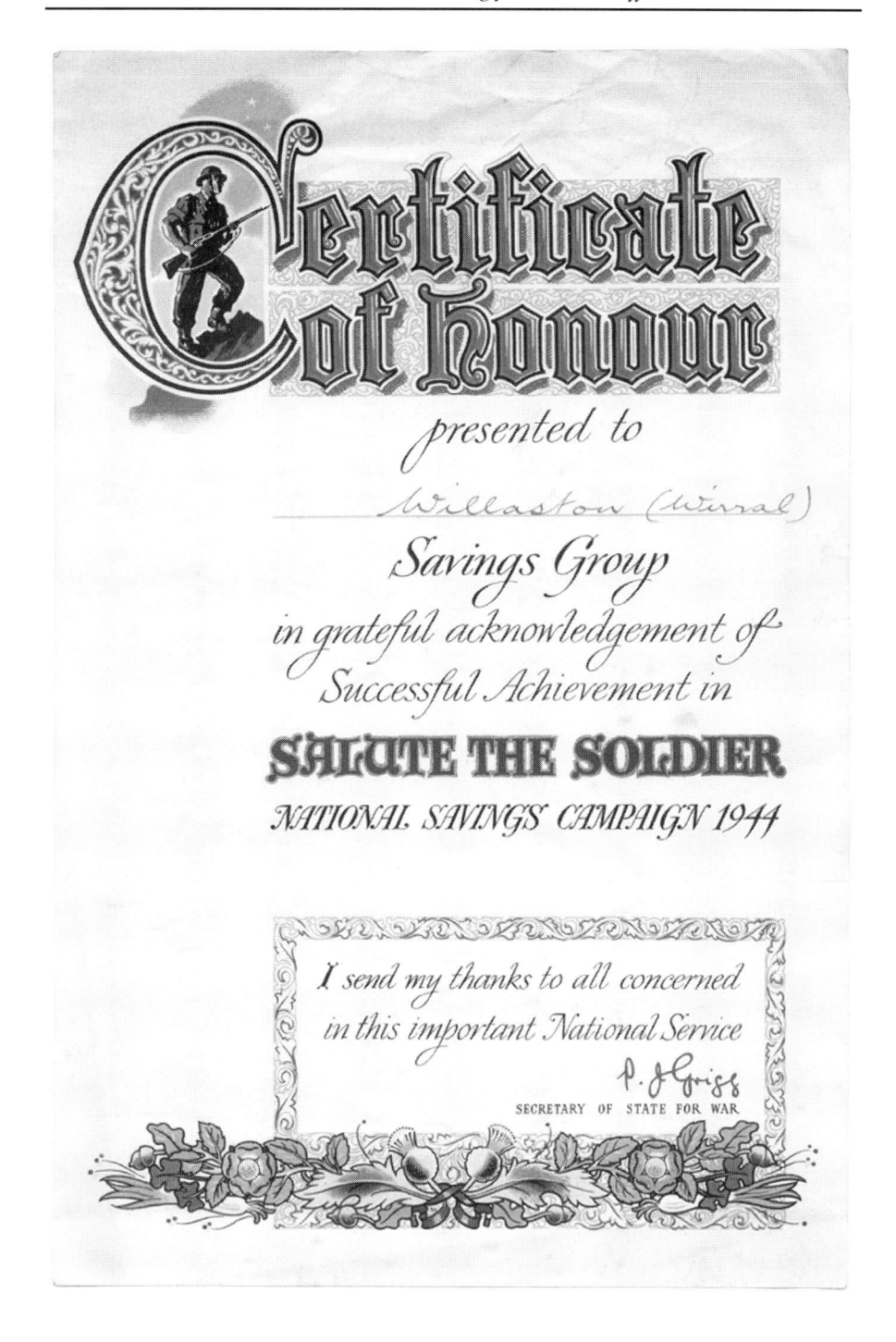

The Home Front: Working for the War Effort

Certificate of honour

presented to

Willaston (Wirral)

Savings Group

in grateful acknowledgement of Successful Achievement in

SALUTE THE SOLDIER

NATIONAL SAVINGS CAMPAIGN 1944

I send my thanks to all concerned in this important National Service

P. J. Grigg

SECRETARY OF STATE FOR WAR

astonishing sums of money were raised: £125,000 locally for War Weapons Week, and £99,000 for Warship Week, when Neston adopted a ship of its own, HM Gunboat *87*. Anyone with spare cash was urged to buy war bonds, and income tax was raised to 50%. The people of Britain had the impression that they were paying for the war, but after the first two years this was an illusion. The country was essentially bankrupt and living on American credit. The sums raised, however, were useful in keeping down inflation by taking the money out of circulation.

Oddly enough, in view of the paper shortage, the war years were a bureaucratic minefield, with innumerable forms to be filled in for many procedures. The first of these was the identity card which everybody was supposed to carry. As the 1943 annual report of the Burton & Puddington WI so feelingly put it,

> *The Pie Scheme admirably illustrates the love of forms that seems bred into the bones of all Ministries, since the Pie Returns have to be made out on 6 different forms and sent to five different places every 8 weeks! If returns are late, back comes another form. Sometimes they even decide they want something quite different.*

One reason for the need to send forms to different places was the decentralization of Government, which placed ministerial offices in each of the regions. In the North-West there was the Ministry of Agriculture at Lytham St Annes, but the County War Ag was at Reaseheath; the Ministry of Supply's Timber Control was in Liverpool, but its Divisional Petroleum Office and Buildings Control were in Manchester; the Iron and Steel Control was still in London; the Ministry of Food was in Colwyn Bay. There was another office of the Ministry of Works in Chester.

The wartime file of Mostyn House is stuffed with forms, official letters, explanatory leaflets and regulations. Just one example of the licences needed is the permit, issued by the Examination Service at the Dock Office, Liverpool, for the school to use its sailing dinghy and outboard motor. At least the rowing boat and sand yachts did not need permits, but they did not escape the war — they were destroyed by an incendiary.

ARP wardens		G. M. Richardson
Fire Guards		Capt. Plummer
Home Guard		Lieut. J. Hargreaves
WVS		Miss Field, Centre organizer
Scouts		J. M. Tomlinson, Major Wilmot Welch
Guides		Miss Barber
Church Lads' Club		Rev. J. Russell Edwards
WI Burton		Mrs Blissett
WI Willaston		Mrs Cox
Salvage stewards		
Rescue team		A. Tillotson
Manual workers		
Schools:	Mostyn House	A. M. D. Grenfell
	Burton Road	A. J. Exton
	St Winefride's	Miss McNeill
	Burton	Miss Fone
	Evacuee	G. Vining
	Little Neston	J. R. Davies
	Liverpool Road	G. H. Fowles
	Willaston	W. J. Helm
National Savings Movement		G. H. Fowles
Water service		H. B. Prince
British Legion		W. G. Haughton
Red Cross		Miss Jackson, J. Hacking, Miss Clayton (ambulance), Mrs Larden Williams (sewing, etc.)
Neston Female Friendly Society		A. Tilley
Ancient Order of Shepherds		J. Cottrell
Royal & Ancient Order of Buffaloes		P. Pickston, J. R. Corkill
Police		Sergeant Eaton
Mortuary		H. Foote
Ministry of Information		H. E. Green (Neston secretary)
Penny-a-Week fund		Mrs Schroder
Billeting officers		Miss Parry

Representatives of local organizations were invited to a "United Nations" Day ceremony in June 1942.

Chapter Eight

SOURCES

This chapter was written by Geoffrey Place.

Susan Chambers researched salvage and savings, and Hilary Morris provided the information about the Women's Institutes.

We are grateful to Ina Bushell for the account of the Neston timber dump (from information given by Reg Bushell and Edgar Gray); to Colin Foote and Bill Jones for their memories of school; and to Kath Bushell, Marie Crook, Julian Grenfell, Clare Johnson, Jim Johnson, Kathleen Kinnaston (née Gray), Graham Langley, Tommy Maddox, Derek Mellor, Emily Oxton, Andrew Prince, Betty Pritchard, Mary Sir (née Scarratt), Arnold Whiteway and David Woodhouse.

CHAPTER NINE

THE ARMED FORCES

Men and women in uniform were a common sight throughout Wirral and a constant reminder that we were at war. Several buildings in the Neston area were requisitioned by the military authorities for the use of troops. Although Parliament had given power for Government to take anything that was needed, if possible requisition was done by agreement. The case of Ashburton, a house in Manorial Road, Parkgate, will serve to illustrate the method.

Ashburton, owned by Daryl Grenfell, was empty after his tenant had left. On 19 June 1940 Major Clegg, the quartering commandant at Chester, wrote to Mr Grenfell enclosing a requisition notice in triplicate, *"as it is understood that you have no objection to the occupation by Military"*. In October the War Department land agent and valuer in Chester sent a form of agreement for the rent, which was fixed at £120 a year, payable quarterly. At the same time a marching-in statement was received from the 38th (Welsh) Division, whose headquarters then occupied the building. But the divisional headquarters moved on very soon, and in January 1941 the Army released the house. Ashburton was at once requisitioned by the Town Clerk of Neston on behalf of the Ministry of Health as a maternity hostel. It would seem, though, that the ministry would pay only £90 per annum in rent.

Grenfell might have been in for a similar experience in August 1939, when part of his field at the end of Bevyl Road was requisitioned for Searchlight Site No.41324, but the requisition was cancelled a year later, in October 1940.

Also in Parkgate was Leighton School, occupying the building that later became the Parkgate Hotel. May Richardson, who had run her girls' school there since about 1918, decided to retire, and closed the school. Throughout the war it was used by Army units, usually for short periods before sailing overseas from Liverpool. The unit best remembered locally was Z Company of the 9th Battalion, Royal Northumberland Fusiliers, because they used to march with their band to church on Sundays. They moved into Leighton School on 15 April 1941, and established the officers' mess at Woodcote, a house in Wood Lane. They were in Parkgate during the May blitz of Liverpool and had to put out a great number of incendiaries. They also took into custody Heinz Dunkerbeck, the German pilot who had baled out over the Dee. William Brown was stationed there:

> *The field between the school and the seashore was used as our training ground, football matches, etc. Other parts of the grounds were used to store ammunition, Molotov cocktails, etc. The area in Boathouse Lane now used as a car saleroom housed some sheds which we used as a small motor transport garage. We didn't have beds — we slept on straw palliasses on the floor and thought nothing of it. Rations were collected from a depot at Saughall near Chester. Being a machine-gun unit we needed to do our training in open country, in North Wales.*
>
> *Off duty we were very well looked after by the good people of Parkgate and Neston. Our favourite spot in Parkgate was probably the Boat House Café, run by the Misses Smith. These two ladies provided beautiful suppers at rock-bottom prices. Another favourite place was the canteen in the church hall at the Presbyterian church in Neston. And of course there were always very good dances in Neston Institute and at the town hall. At that time the swimming pool in Parkgate was still open and was very much enjoyed by all when duties permitted.*

Reg Bushell and his friends used to go and watch the soldiers on their assault course and bayonet practice ground behind the school. So did Tommy Maddox, who lived in a cottage in the grounds: *"Daily drilling of soldiers in Wood Lane afforded much amusement to locals because of their ill-fitting uniforms."* But after seven months at Parkgate, Z Company moved to Birkenhead and the whole battalion sailed on the *Warwick Castle* to Singapore. They had only just arrived when the island fell to the Japanese and they became prisoners of war.

The Northumberland Fusiliers were followed by B Company of the 5th Battalion, Cheshire Regiment, who arrived from Northern Ireland. Like their predecessors, they were allowed free use of Neston Town Hall for a company dance. Later some men from the Green Howards were remembered at Leighton School. In 1944 it seems likely that some men from the Cheshire (Earl of Chester's) Yeomanry were also billeted at Leighton School. Their regimental history states that they were *"at Grenfell's"* (Mostyn House), but this is thought to be a mistake.

Another empty building requisitioned by the Army was Ashfield Hall, off the Chester High Road. C Company of the 4th Battalion, Cheshire

The Armed Forces

Ashfield Hall (*top*) is now a barn. During the war, it was occupied by the Army and then used to store aircraft parts. However, it was not until the 1950s that the house and its out-buildings (*below*) reached the sorry state that they present today.

Regiment, was billeted there in September 1939. Other units remembered there include some Royal Artillery and No.60 Railway Construction Company of the Royal Engineers. The Army had left the hall before Karl Jennings arrived at the farm on 16 April 1942. The Ministry of Aircraft Production took over the hall and used it to store aircraft parts for Vickers-Armstrong. Mr Jennings had to see that fire buckets were always filled with water or sand in case of incendiary bombs.

Soldiers were also billeted in Thornton Hough at the Lever school and Westwood Grange, and at Burton Manor. The 4th Cheshires were spread among all three houses, as well as Ashfield Hall, in 1939. Brian Danger was there and was impressed by the hard floors he had to sleep on at Burton Manor. He remembers that Sir John Nicholson, who lived at Parkgate, and Denis Vosper, a future Government minister, were officers there. Another was Captain Kenneth Lucking, a Territorial officer who was playing cricket at Parkgate when his call-up notice came. He is said to have asked the bowler for a suitable farewell ball, hit it for six and left Neston for ever. He was killed in action in Belgium on 19 May 1940. The battalion was later at Dunkirk and some were captured. Burton Manor was later taken over by Western Command, which was based at Chester, and it became the regional headquarters of the NAAFI (Navy, Army & Air Force Institutes), which provided canteens for the services. Girls were recruited to work there from as far afield as Liverpool, Manchester and Salford, and they lived in at the Manor if they could not get home. In April 1944 the Western Command supervisor appealed to Neston Council for help with *"the Rat Menace around Burton Manor"*.

The Lever school was occupied by the Army, and the purpose of the soldiers there was to maintain the Army vehicles which were parked the whole length of all the non-public Lever estate roads. They were solid from Thornton Hough to Storeton and from the Manor to the gates where there is now a motorway roundabout.

Some years ago, Mrs Jean Robinson (née Bromilow) of Neston revisited Hereford, where she had been Manageress of the NAAFI throughout the war. She was decorated by General de Gaulle.

Further afield, there were military hospitals at Eaton Hall and Moston, with a retraining centre for injured servicemen at the Dales camp nearby. The RAF had a training camp at West Kirby and, as already stated, were using airfields at Hooton Park, Little Sutton, Sealand, Hawarden and Poulton. In October 1941 the RAF station at Hooton Park offered to put on a two-hour concert in Neston in aid of the RAF Benevolent Fund. Army recruits were trained at Saighton and Arrowe Park, with the headquarters of Western Command at Chester Castle. When Liverpool became the headquarters of Western Approaches, where the long battle against German submarines was fought, there was a considerable naval presence as well. Over four and a half million servicemen sailed into or out of Liverpool during the war. Commander R. E. Rankin lived in Wood Lane, Parkgate, and several senior officers from Liverpool came to stay with him to seek relaxation.

The Royal Navy eventually came to Neston in the form of a shore establishment called HMS *Mersey*, on land at Clayhill, to the north of Liverpool Road. Twenty-two acres of this land had been requisitioned in 1942 by the Ministry of Health to provide hostels for those made homeless by the bombing. Altogether 37 brick huts and fourteen precast concrete buildings were built there by the end of the war. They were not actually used for people bombed out of Merseyside, but were employed briefly as an Army camp and then as a clearing station for Gibraltarians. From September 1944 these 'National Service Hostels' were occupied by families from London who were escaping the flying bomb attacks.

HMS *Mersey* was established as a depot for merchant seamen who were serving as volunteers or conscripts in the Royal Navy — known in naval jargon as 'T.124X personnel'. The depot was set up in 1940 beside the Liverpool docks, in the building of the David Lewis Northern Hospital. HMS *Mersey* remained by the docks until the war was over; then, on 3 December 1945, it moved to Neston. However, the Navy stayed for no more than six months; the camp closed in July 1946 and was officially paid off in December.

HMS *Mersey* was actually used in its Neston period as a point of demobilization for sailors returning home. One of these was James Palmer, who was paid and demobbed on 18 December 1945. He celebrated with three friends in a pub in Parkgate, where he met Moreen Branagan. Moreen, aged 31, worked as a barmaid at the Holywell Hotel in Parkgate, but she had not been at work that day. She had been shopping in Liverpool and had met Palmer on the bus back. At 7.30 p.m.

she and Palmer went to Neston and spent the rest of the evening in the Brewer's Arms, although she was engaged to marry someone else. At closing time, after drinking port with beer chasers, they walked down to Wood Lane. In Palmer's own words,

> We were kissing and this seemed to arouse me. We fell on the roadway. I fell on top of her and intimacy took place. She slapped my face and said, 'You shouldn't have done that', and started squirming on the ground and screaming. She was throwing her hands about in a claw-like manner and I tried to catch hold of them. I did not know I had struck her at all. She seemed to go limp and her struggles ceased.

Moreen was dead. Palmer left her there and fled to Glasgow. Early the next morning, Molly Roberts was cycling through Neston on her way to work at a house in Wood Lane when she met Monk Jones. Monk, whose real name was Sam, was boatman to Harold Gill, the wildfowler. "Not to worry, love," said Monk, "when you go down Wood Lane you will see a little girl on the ground; she has been knocked off her bike." She saw Moreen on the ground and went on to tell her employer, Commander Rankin, who went out in his dressing gown and wellingtons to investigate. But the police had already been alerted by Geoffrey Groundsell, who lived nearby and had discovered the body on his early morning walk. Moreen was lying opposite Roseacre, just short of Parks Field. The house Frankland was built there in 1961, and when its owner later saw the pathologist's photograph of the body, what struck her was that Moreen was wearing court shoes with ankle socks.

Palmer was arrested and tried for murder. Moreen had died of suffocation and bruising of the thyroid gland, but the pathologist agreed that she was a frail woman, six and a half stone and five feet two, pigeon chested with chronic pleurisy. People in Neston seem to have thought that her death was bad luck and a petition was circulated on Palmer's behalf. He was found guilty and sentenced to death, but three days before the execution he was reprieved and served nine years in prison.

Some local people saw a great deal of the servicemen. Some of the young pilots training at Sealand used to come to Parkgate to shoot wildfowl on the marsh for relaxation, and they met at the Watch House where the Bushells lived.

> They used to leave their shotguns stacked in the big oak corner cupboard and my dad would keep them clean and oiled. Our house always seemed full in those days — there were always men there, collecting their shotguns or bringing them back after a day's shooting, discussing the day's sport or the

news from the war fronts. There would be men leaning on the doorways and windowsills, perched on the stone staircase, draped on the chairs, with my mother constantly going in and out with cups of tea.

One pilot buzzed the Bushells' fishing boat with his plane and actually hit the mast.

Soldiers off duty often played football with the locals. When three schoolboys were playing football beside Burton Road and some soldiers joined in, they were thrilled to learn that one of them was Frank Soo, an England and Stoke City professional.

Dances were a very popular evening entertainment at the time.

Several Parkgate mothers considered that roving soldiers with little to occupy their spare time could be troublesome, so they organized dances in Rigby House at 6d. a hop. The mothers did teas and firmly rejected unsuitable girls.

A band called the Rigby Boys was formed in 1943 to play at these dances, and also at Neston Institute, the Oddfellows Hall in Ness and at Burton Manor. The players were Frank Clarke (alto saxophone), Stan Robinson (accordion), Laurie Davies (piano), Roy Booth (clarinet) and Dickie Price followed by Tom Maddox on drums.

The United States entered the war in December 1942 after the Japanese attacked their Pacific fleet at Pearl Harbor. Germany and Italy, who had a pact with Japan, at once declared war on the USA. The conflict was now truly a world war, and the scales of power began to tilt firmly against Hitler. American servicemen began to be seen in the Neston area after a camp for them was set up on Bromborough golf course. A military hospital for the Americans was established at Clatterbridge in 1944, using some huts formerly used as a British emergency hospital, with extra buildings erected on 25 acres of land taken from Grange Farm. General Patton visited the hospital, which was in use for less than a year. Graham Langley watched the American military police touring the villages to round up GIs who were the worse for drink. His father heard American soldiers singing at a harvest festival at Thornton Hough Congregational church in October 1944.

The first prisoners of war to be seen locally were Italians who were housed at Sylvandale, Spital Road, Bromborough. They probably came there in 1943, as before that Wirral was marked on official maps as being unsuitable for prisoner-of-war camps — too near the docks, no doubt. When Italy, faced with invasion, made peace with the Allies and declared war on Germany in September 1943, her soldiers were no longer our enemies. They were employed on farms in the Raby and Clatterbridge area, and Neston pupils of Wirral Grammar School used to see them as they cycled to school. When they returned they would see the Italians sitting on a bank, waiting for a truck to take them back to camp, and would chat to some of them. They wore army uniforms with large coloured patches on the back. They were not given any wages, and a truck driver from Neston called John Bailey, who worked for a Raby farmer, teased these Italians by saying that he got paid for his work. *"You wunna be drawing very much, then!"* was the reply. One Neston man, Tom Taylor, was reported in October 1943 to be a guard for POWs *"quite near Neston"*. Two of the Italians stayed on after the war and married local girls. One of them used to live in Raby.

In the autumn of 1944, German prisoners were housed at Ledsham Hall camp, previously used by British troops and then briefly by Americans. Wilson's Transport of Ledsham, the main milk and dairy feed carriers in the area, had the contract to take them to local farms in a canvas-topped lorry. The camp housed about two hundred Germans in Nissen huts. It took some years after the war to resettle the Germans in their own country, and some remained until 1949–50.

Reg Bushell recorded that some prisoners of war were billeted at a house at Hooton, opposite the Roften factory. For a short time after the war, some were housed at Clatterbridge in buildings vacated by the American military hospital.

> *The Germans kept themselves apart from the Italians, and were always clean-shaven and neat despite their rough clothes, whereas the Italians always seemed to be sloppy and unkempt. When the lorries came to collect them, the Germans would line up and march as a squad. We had to admire the discipline of the Germans, though they were our enemies.*

Usually the Germans did farm work, but Major Higgin at Puddington Hall employed one German as a cook and another as his valet. Reg Bushell did repairs at that farm: *"We used to offer the prisoners some of our sandwiches, because they had very meagre rations from the camp, but the Germans were very proud and would never accept food from us."*

Some of the men used to carve objects like cigarette boxes, with even the hinges carved from wood. These they used to sell to the locals. A prisoner at Raby used to make slippers out of webbing and hawk them. One man showed the 16-year-old Reg Bushell a picture of his wife and family: *"They didn't seem so very different from us."*

When George Langley wanted some German prisoners to work on his farm, he went personally to the camp at Ledsham, and the next day, 6 May 1946, two men came. He employed two prisoners, occasionally three, for most of the rest of the year, and started them again in May 1947. He was not allowed to pay them or give them cigarettes, but *"this was done quietly"*. The numbers employed by farmers varied with seasonal needs. Geoff Nicholls once had twenty Germans lifting potatoes.

One Christmas the local people were asked to have a prisoner in their homes for the day. Vera Bridgewater's mother, Mrs White, invited two Germans, even though her husband was away fighting their countrymen. They were called Max and Joseph and they brought with them a German Christmas cake. After tea, Joseph played the piano and everyone sang carols, with the visitors singing 'Silent Night' in German. When Mr White came home on leave he was pleased that his family had entertained the Germans.

The German who worked on the Crossleys' market garden in 1945, Joseph Krauthausen, was a staunch supporter of Hitler, but he was a good worker and gave the children Christmas presents which he made himself — a model of a Lancaster bomber, a rocking horse, and a chicken pecking game. The next German they had, Erwin Winter, was totally different, a quiet, studious man opposed to Hitler.

The prisoners of war clearly made a considerable impression on the civilians they met. Two of those employed at Ashfield Hall Farm by Karl Jennings came back to see him from Germany, with their families, some years later.

The most welcome uniforms to be seen in Neston were, of course, those of servicemen or women on leave. It is not possible to state how many people from Neston served in the armed forces, but at the end of 1945 it was reported that 650 were still in the forces from the Neston area (Neston and Parkgate, Little Neston, Ness, Burton and Willaston). To that figure should be added the 82 who had died on active service. The doings of some of them can be glimpsed in a series of monthly letters written between 1941 and 1945 by the curate of Neston, J. Russell Edwards. He wrote a total of 44 duplicated letters, and by January 1945 he was posting 130 copies of each issue to the former members of his Church Lads' Club. Russell Edwards (Jack to his family but 'the Boss' to his correspondents) had become curate of Neston in 1935. Although he left in 1943 to be vicar of Congleton, he continued to edit the Neston newsletter. From 1948 until his retirement in 1983 he was vicar of Dunham Massey.

Chapter Nine

The Rev. J. Russell Edwards and members of the Church Lads' Club, in Comrades Field, Neston, in 1939. *L. to r: back row*, Ron Ashton, Arthur Rossiter, Harold Tozer, George Hill, Bill Astbury, Noel Jordan, Alan Cotterell, Ewart Lee, Ken Lane, Arthur Bartley, Peter Ludden, Jack Millington, Bill Rowlands; *middle row*, Ben Carruthers, Ray Johnson, Les Bell, Bill Lowndes, Duncan Jamieson, Rev. Russell Edwards, Tom Hughes, Frank Stallard, Herbert Wragg, Jim Bartley, Gwillam Evans; *front row*, Harold Johnson, Cyril (Ciggi) Bell, Clarence Pyke.

The letters give almost no news at all of Neston itself. One of the few exceptions is in July 1941, when *"a contractor is removing 25,000 tons of spoil from the colliery tips, making the place look quite different."* Apparently this spoil was taken to New Ferry to protect and conceal a fuel tank built close to the shore. The same letter reports that *"the sands at Parkgate are looking more like marsh as the plants spread towards the Boat House."* Otherwise the letters chiefly give such limited news of the correspondents as the military censors would allow. *"I find that we must have a humorist in the censor's office. Roger Stallard tells me that one of his letters had the envelope stamped with the word 'Propaganda'."* One writer, who said that there was *"good stuff"*, meaning girls, in Llandudno, had the town's name obliterated by the censor, who knew that Llandudno was a centre for radar research. Somebody wrote, *"I can't tell you where I am but there are pyramids at the bottom of the garden."*

'Nessoners' seem to have served in almost every corner of the globe. Letters were received from Egypt and North Africa, Gibraltar, East, West

The Armed Forces

Edgar Dodd, Vida Jackson, Jess Rodgers and Ewart Warburton, representing some of the different branches of the Services, survived the war.

Neston Territorials at camp in the early days of the war. They include Ernest Smith, Bill Roscoe, Peter Cottrell, Alf Kerrigan, Albert (Leggie) Sharp and Joe Young.

and South Africa, India, Ceylon, Burma, Thailand, Singapore, USA, Canada, Malta, Greece, Italy, France, Holland, Luxembourg, Germany, Iceland and Australia. They also came from every part of the United Kingdom. Quite often, people from Neston met in surprising places: Roy Bailey had a pleasant surprise when he met Ronald Benbow in a cinema in Colombo.

The letters are mostly gossip and say little about what people were actually doing. But four decorations are reported: Ward Gunn's Victoria Cross, the Military Medal awarded for gallantry to Tom Bostock, the Dutch medal given to Tom's brother-in-law George Rigby for his service with the Royal Netherlands Navy, and Joe Alexander's Distinguished Service Medal awarded *"for sticking to his guns in a sticky encounter"*. People are named as missing, or sometimes as prisoners or as killed. Three prisoners of war managed to escape: Ted Pearson escaped from northern Italy to Switzerland, and Stephen Sharps also escaped from a camp in Italy. But Ray Peters

> *landed a trifle out of his right place in France and after dodging about for a few days, he was taken prisoner. The sentry was not sharp enough and suffered for*

it. Ray and six others made a dash for it; only three were successful, and Ray was one of them.

Being originally for a 'lads' club', the letters rarely mention women in the forces, but three are named: Joy Pearson in the ATS, Poppy Anyon and Joan Morgan in the WRNS.

Russell Edwards was not, of course, the only person writing to members of the forces. He reported that in 1945 *"the Neston CCNS have sent out over 5,000 letters"*. (We are not sure what these initials stand for: could it be the Committee for Corresponding with National Servicemen?)

Occasionally Neston people would encounter those who refused military service on grounds of moral principle — the conscientious objectors. One of these was Henry Coomber, who lived in Wood Lane, Parkgate. He had attended a Quaker school and felt that he could not accept a fighting role. He had to attend a tribunal in Liverpool, chaired by a judge, to justify his case. If the tribunal agreed that the objector was sincere, they could find him work, often in agriculture, or as a non-combatant in the services, such as medical work. If the tribunal found him insincere he could be ordered to accept call-up or, in cases of extreme intransigence, be sent to prison. Mr Coomber found his examination a frightening experience, but the tribunal granted him exemption and he was sent to work on a fruit farm in Puddington. The farmer took the view that Mr Coomber's beliefs were his own business, but his neighbours were by no means so tolerant.

One conscientious objector, Tom Jones, worked on George Langley's farm in Raby. He is remembered for having given a pint of blood twice a year. Another was billeted on the Grantham family in Moorside Lane and given the job of clearing two acres of overgrown land with an axe, but he was not fit enough to do the work. Horby Exton, a son of the belligerently patriotic headmaster of Neston council school in Burton Road, was also a conscientious objector, but he volunteered to serve in the forces as a non-combatant medical orderly. He was taken prisoner in 1941 (as reported in Russell Edwards's August newsletter) and did not return home until four years later, in June 1945.

It is scarcely possible to do justice to the varied experiences of those who served in the armed forces. Therefore a handful of accounts have been chosen which may go some way to represent the service of hundreds of others.

Joseph Davies, whose parents lived in Mayfield Gardens, joined the Army in 1937. He was stationed at Singapore before the war started, and

Chapter Nine

when the Japanese captured the island in February 1942, Corporal Davies and 70,000 other troops were ordered to surrender. Many of them were mustered on the beach, where, under Japanese machine-guns, they piled their weapons and waited to be taken to prisoner-of-war camps. Joe later told this story to a *Daily Mail* reporter:

Suddenly, near the surf, seven men dashed from the ranks, raced across the sands and waded off to a Chinese junk. A few bullets kicked up spray as they fell short of the men. With the aid of a compass and the stars they decided to sail for Sumatra. For five days they sailed, being lucky to escape notice by Japanese planes and patrol boats. When they reached Sumatra they learned that the Japanese had invaded it; they marched through jungle and gorges and across mountains. The survivors managed to board a destroyer just ahead of the enemy.

Davies was taken to Java and then to India, where he recovered in hospital at Poona. Joe Davies returned home on leave in 1943 but then took part in the invasion of Europe. In October 1944 he was reported killed in action in Holland.

By contrast, Henry Peters spent a much less exciting but a very busy war, a vital part of the support services for the front-line troops. He was called up in 1940 and became an RASC driver in Number Four Petrol Depot. He sailed from Liverpool in February 1941 on a long voyage of eleven weeks,

A reminder that the USA also had a military presence in the area. Nellie Sowden was the bridesmaid when this wedding took place at Little Neston Methodist chapel.

all the way round Africa to Port Said in Egypt. There were 2,000 men on the ship, the *Ascanius*. There was very little water, and washing arrangements were primitive. Henry and his unit then moved to the Shell refinery at Haifa, and it was their job to look after petrol dumps scattered throughout Palestine, often in orange groves. They had to change the stock in their dumps regularly to keep it up to grade, and petrol was shipped to various places in the Mediterranean, such as Cyprus. Henry drove his lorry for hundreds of miles throughout Palestine, Jordan and Syria. When a big push was planned, *"we were never in bed but hard at it night and day."*

Number Four Petrol Unit was then sent to Italy to service a petrol dump at Brindisi, later moving north to Ancona, where they had to restore the railway after the Germans had wrecked it. Just as the war in Europe ended they entered Venice. He returned to Britain in June 1945, in another very crowded ship, and was finally demobbed in November.

Jim Anyon had been a Sea Scout in Neston and was determined to join the Royal Navy. To make sure of this he enrolled in the RNVR, with several friends, six months before the war started. He was called up as soon as war was declared and sent to Plymouth, and then sailed to Gibraltar in a passenger liner. He fared much better than Henry Peters because the ship had not been stripped for war and the cabins were luxurious. At Gibraltar he and Fred Beckett, also from Neston, joined HMS *Galatea*, a light cruiser. This ship's task was to stop merchant vessels and search for contraband — materials useful to the enemy. If they found contraband, a skeleton crew would take the ship to the nearest port. American ships, neutral at that date, were well equipped and generous, so they would stop one deliberately in the hope of a good meal.

Jim left *Galatea* to take a gun-layer's course at Alexandria. Then he was posted to HMS *Aphis*, a 'China river gunboat', so called to conceal its real purpose, to operate in rivers or shallows nearer home. The ship drew only 3fi feet of water and so could sail close to the North African shore, where it fired its guns, two 3-inch and two 6-inch, in support of the Eighth Army. When *Aphis* called at Tobruk, Jim met another Neston man, Herbert Fairclough. The day after *Aphis* sailed away, Tobruk fell and Sergeant Fairclough was taken prisoner; his capture was reported by Russell Edwards in July 1942. The *Aphis* was away from base for three months at a time: *"The ship was full of rats and I slept on deck with a rat trap on either side of me. I threw the rats overboard each morning."* Another problem was water, as each man was allowed one pint a day for all

Chapter Nine

HMS *Aphis*, the 'China river gunboat' in which Jim Anyon served for two years off North Africa.

purposes. Tea was made with half salt water, half fresh, and had a half-inch scum on top. The only way to keep clean was to dive overboard. The work was risky and the crew received extra allowances because of the difficult conditions. Jim served on *Aphis* for over two years but came home on a minesweeper in December 1943.

He then qualified as a Leading Seaman, and while on an exercise he fired his 3-inch gun at a drogue towed by an aircraft. Jim hit the target in the centre and two pieces came floating down. *"I've never seen that done before"*, said the captain. *"You'll never see it again, sir"*, said Jim. When he returned to Neston, the only man there on leave on D-Day, he was glad to see his own bed after nearly five years away. He was able to visit his sister, who was a Wren in the Isle of Man. Jim remained in the Navy after the war.

Albert (Abbie) Peters was also in the Royal Navy. He was killed in action south-east of Crete. His ship, the destroyer *Juno*, had engaged six German E-boats during the night and then suffered a four-hour attack by planes. She was hit by bombs about 1 p.m. on 21 May 1941 and broke in half. She sank in 60 seconds. Another Neston sailor to die was Neville Scott, lost on a convoy to Murmansk, his first and last voyage.

The Armed Forces

Top left, Lieut. Harry Glyn, RN, from Moorside (seen here as a midshipman), died at Narvik in 1940. *Top right*, Ralph Jellicoe, of the Royal Marines, was killed when returning from the Normandy beaches in July 1944. *Bottom left*, Albert Peters lost his life when his ship was sunk in May 1941. *Bottom right*, Ron Wyke, a radio officer in the Merchant Navy, was also killed.

Chapter Nine

Cissie Lee was a Wren. She volunteered for the Women's Royal Naval Service in 1941, a few months before her eighteenth birthday, because she wanted to get away from Neston and see a bit of life. She spent her first eighteen months at Pwllheli, and was then sent on a course in London to train as a writer. Normally Wrens were required to go out in pairs when they left their quarters, but during the blitz they had to go in sixes, supervised by a Petty Officer. After a posting to a submarine base at Cardiff, she spent two and a half years at Greenock attached to the Canadian navy. There was plenty of social life, and for Cissie the war years were the best time of her life.

Jack Worthington is an example of those who fought with the RAF. He joined up before the war because there was very little work available locally. He qualified as a wireless operator but undertook other duties in the bombers that he served in, including acting as gunner and navigator. When war broke out he was posted to 99 Squadron, which had Wellington bombers. His first duty was to drop leaflets and then do reconnaissance work, looking for German ships in the Heligoland Bight. In December 1939 the squadron was doing shipping sweeps in the North Sea. In June 1940, just before France surrendered, the squadron was sent to Salon, an airfield in the South of France, in order to bomb Italy, which was too far to reach from Britain. Italy had declared war on the Allies on 10 June. Jack still has his log book, which shows that he was bombing Genoa and Milan, for which he was mentioned in despatches. When France fell and the squadron returned to England, Jack had to *"get out of a plane in a hurry"*, and after this crash he was not allowed to fly again because he was not fit enough. He served as a ground instructor for the rest of the war.

Jack married during the war, and his wife Margaret came to Neston in 1941 but moved about the country with her husband. At the end of the war her mother-in-law said she had found her a flat, and she returned to Neston to look. It turned out to be a Nissen hut at Puddington, but she turned it down because it was too quiet and nowhere near the shops.

Bill Scarratt was a member of the 'Forgotten Army' which defeated the Japanese in Burma. He went first to France with the King's Own Royal Regiment at Rouen. When the Germans invaded, the order came to get out quickly, which was not easy when every road was jammed with fleeing soldiers and civilians. Bill got away on a ship from Le Havre, exhausted. He was then transferred to the Lancashire Fusiliers, guarding the east coast near Hull. On an exercise they had to cross a river, and Bill's boat collapsed: six men were drowned and only three saved. In 1942 he was sent to India with the Lancashire Fusiliers. On the way he was in a bar in Capetown when he heard a Neston voice say, *"Hey youse!"* It was Bill Ireland, who was in the Navy. In India his unit was used to support the civil power, by facing rioters in Bombay — *"Fixed bayonets are not much use against thousands"* — and rounding up bandits in the north.

In 1944 Bill Scarratt flew from Madras to Burma, where he fought in the battle of Kohima, one of the pivotal battles of the war. It was the monsoon season and the mud came almost to the top of their legs. They slept where they could, in a trench or under a corrugated-iron sheet. They ate what they could carry, mainly bully beef and biscuits, and water was always a problem. The troops had to suffer dysentery, beriberi, malaria, typhus and inadequate medical facilities, though the medics did all they could. In the battle of Kohima (*"more shells than at Alamein"*) the opposing forces were only a hundred yards apart. At night the Japs would call out, *"Come on, Johnny, come over here, we've got your mate"*, but the orders were not to respond, as it was a device to ascertain their positions. At one point, Bill's company was stuck on top of a hill, marooned by Japanese who charged point-blank in the teeth of fire. They took few prisoners, as the Japanese would rather die than surrender. During the battle, supplies were dropped by Dakotas, which sometimes missed their mark, and the men had to go into the jungle to retrieve the food and ammunition, very frightening and *"hairy"*.

After the first engagement Bill, then a sergeant, had to lead men to the dead bodies to retrieve personal belongings and identity discs. The bodies were then dragged by ropes for temporary burial, to be exhumed and reburied later. The Japs sometimes booby-trapped bodies by leaving a grenade underneath. Our wounded were carried to a mobile hospital down jungle tracks, impenetrable to British troops who did not know the way, by a local hill tribe, the Nagas, who hated the Japs for their cruelty.

The Japanese retreated to Imphal, where another battle was fought, after which only 27 able men were left out of 130 in Bill's company. But they had to fight and win a third battle, at Mandalay, before they could rest. Bill ended the war as a sergeant-major and landed in England in November 1945, shivering in the cold after three years in the tropics.

The huge quantities of mail which passed between Britain and members of the services abroad was a problem because it took up so much valuable space in aircraft. One solution was the airgraph, a small sheet allowing a brief letter which was microfilmed and then printed out at the other end.

Chapter Nine

An example of a letter from North Africa is this one, written by Lance-Corporal Jack Wheeler of the Royal Tank Regiment in February 1942:

Dear Mother,

Many thanks for your cards which arrive pretty regularly, also papers. Have not received George's photo yet or heard from him. We are getting quite a good rest which is a change. I heard from Mr Edwards recently, and from what you write between you, Neston appears to be the same. As you say I would very much like to see it again.

Love to all, your loving son, Jack.

Jack Wheeler was killed in action, reported by Russell Edwards in November 1943.

Jack Wheeler, well known in local sports circles, was serving with the Royal Tank Regiment when he was reported killed in November 1943.

The dreaded official letter or telegram brought a steady stream of bad news throughout the war. When Harry Bartley was captured in June 1942, the pre-printed letter from the Army Record Office stated:

I regret to have to inform you that a report has been received from the War Office to the effect that No.2593597 Cpl Bartley H. C., Royal Corps of Signals, was posted as 'missing' on 29.6.42.

The news that he was a prisoner of war came through two months later.

The first Neston serviceman to be reported killed was Albert Prince. He had joined the RAF before the war, in 1935 or 1936, and was a sergeant-pilot flying a Blenheim when he was shot down on the very first day of the war. He had been raiding the German fleet in the Kiel Canal. Surviving members of his crew sent his family some photographs taken at his funeral.

Most of you will have heard the piece of news [wrote Russell Edwards] *of which Nestonians are particularly proud, the award of the VC to Ward Gunn. I think that almost everybody I have met has spoken about it with bright eyes. It was awarded posthumously for great gallantry at Sidi Rezegh.*

The Armed Forces

Sgt Pilot Albert Prince was shot down over Germany on the first day of the war. Here the Union Flag can be glimpsed as naval ratings carry his coffin at his funeral, which was conducted by the German Navy.

Ward Gunn was the son of Dr George Gunn, a local doctor, and went to Mostyn House School before going on to Sedbergh, and he then qualified as a chartered accountant. He volunteered for the army in 1939 and went to North Africa as a Second Lieutenant with the Royal Horse Artillery. His bravery was first recognized at Tobruk, when he was awarded the Military Cross

> *for sustained gallantry and coolness, which inspired all ranks under heavy and close enemy fire, particularly on January 4th and 5th 1941, as one of the heroic Tobruk garrison.*

Ten months later, Ward Gunn, commanding a troop of four field guns, was part of the defence of Sidi Rezegh in Libya against an attack by about sixty German tanks. His guns were knocked out of action one by one until only one was left, with a single man of its crew alive and its trailer on fire. Ward Gunn himself sighted the gun, with his sergeant loading it, and fired forty or fifty shells, knocking out or damaging several enemy tanks at a range of 800 yards. He fell dead, shot through the forehead.

> *He showed the most conspicuous courage in attacking this large number of enemy tanks with a single unarmoured gun, and his utter disregard for extreme danger was an example which inspired all who saw it. He remained undismayed by intense fire and overwhelming odds, and his gallantry only ceased with his death. But for his very gallant action the enemy tanks would undoubtedly have overrun our position.*

The appeal in his memory, already described, raised three times the £500 asked for, and endowed a bed at the cottage hospital. When that closed in 1964 the plaque was placed on a wall of Neston parish church.

Eighty-two men and women from the Neston district died on active service. There are 61 names recorded in Neston parish church, 11 in Burton and 9 in Willaston. To these names may be added that of Lieut. H. T. D. Glynn, RN, who was killed at Narvik aboard HMS *Kimberley* in 1940.

From Burton:

William Biggs
George Capstick
Kenneth Fowden
Reginald Fernyhough
William Howard
Geoffrey Hughes
Edward S. Jones
James E. O'Connell
William Pollard
Arthur Ll. Williams
Raymond E. Williams

From Willaston:

E. P. Bates
K. P. Clayton
A. R. J. Medcalf
F. Parfitt
G. W. Parrott
J. Percival
M. Smyth
H. R. Todd
T. Wood

From Neston, the names recorded at the unveiling of the war memorial in 1954:

FO R. S. Anyon	Pte E. Griffiths	Pte J. Mason
Dvr A. Ashington	Tpr R. A. Griffiths	Bdr R. Metcalfe
Sgt R. Ashton	2/Lt. G. W. Gunn, VC, MC	Janet Peel
Pte J. O. Bartley	Maj. P. McL. Gunn	Pte F. Peers
AC E. Bates	Pte A. Hare	Pte J. H. Peers
C/Eng. W. L. Bee	Sgt/P R. G. Hill	AB A. Peters
OS A. V. Bennett	AB J. E. Holmes	Sgt/P A. S. Prince
Pte H. H. Boyd	RM R. G. Jellicoe	Sister M. Robinson
Maj. R. W. Carrigan, MC	Stkr J. W. Johnson	OS N. Scott
Sgt P. R. Cattrall	Dvr R. M. Johnson	LAC C. V. Smith
Sgt T. W. Coy	L/Cpl A. Jones	Pte L. Smith
Col. K. Crawford	Cpl C. G. Jones	Pte R. Smith
Cpl J. Davies	Pte D. H. Jones	Sgt J. B. Sowden
Sgt J. R. Davies	Pte T. J. Jones	PO P. Swanborough
M/S S. W. Dudley	Maj. J. M. Kenion	Gnr S. A. Wellings
PO R. T. H. Ellis	Pte D. W. Lane	Cpl J. Wheeler
Pte S. Ellis	Capt. W. Lees Evans	Bdr J. R. Wilde
Pte J. Evans	Capt. K. S. B. Lucking	AB R. A. Williams
Capt. R. C. N. Forsyth	Gnr F. J. Lunt	Rad/O T. R. Wyke
Dvr O. A. Goldsmith	Lt. H. W. Marr	
L/Cpl W. P. Goulding	OS E. Mason	

To these should be added the name of Lieut. H. T. D. Glynn, RN

The Great Sacrifice, 1939–1945

Chapter Nine

SOURCES

This chapter was written by Geoffrey Place.

The archives of Mostyn House School were made available by A. D. J. Grenfell.

Useful information was obtained from the war diaries of the Royal Northumberland Fusiliers and the Cheshire Regiment; the regimental histories of the Cheshire Regiment and the Cheshire Yeomanry; and *The Neston Lads' Club News Sheet*, by J. Russell Edwards.

Details of the murder of Moreen Branagan were obtained from Steve Fielding, *Cheshire Murder Casebook* (1996).

We are grateful for the memories of Jack Anyon, Roy Booth, Vera Bridgewater, William Brown, Reg and Ina Bushell, Brian Danger, Colin Foote, Muriel Grantham, Karl Jennings, Graham Langley, Cissie Lee, Tommy Maddox, Geoff Nicholls, Henry Peters, Judith Pugh, Mrs Joyce Russell Edwards, Bill Scarratt, Muriel Tompkins, Joseph Wilson and Jack Worthington.

CHAPTER TEN

PEACE AT LAST

It was chiefly the radio which kept the people of Britain in touch with the progress of the war, and Neston people, like everyone else, heard the stirring speeches of Winston Churchill, and then, all too slowly, the turning points of the war: our victory over the German *Afrika Korps* at El Alamein in the autumn of 1942; the Russian victory at Stalingrad in February 1943, which began the rolling back of the German army, even to Berlin itself; the long-awaited Allied landings on the Normandy beaches on 6 June 1944. If anyone still doubted that the unconditional surrender of Nazi Germany was necessary, the news of the horrors of Belsen Concentration Camp, liberated by British forces in April 1945, should have opened their eyes. One of the voices heard on the radio was that of Wilfrid Grant, a local man who took part in a Christmas broadcast of greetings from East Africa. He expressed that longing, felt by all the absent servicemen, for peace and a return to their families, in a poem addressed to his daughter:

When my daddy comes home what a day that will be,
I'll welcome him home with a smile.
The bands will be playing, the flags flying free,
There'll be laughter and dancing for you and for me.
So let's shout 'Hip, hoorah!' for the land of the free,
When my daddy comes home.

General Montgomery received the surrender of the German forces in north-west Europe on 5 May 1945, and the remaining German forces surrendered two days later. On 8 and 9 May, Britain celebrated Victory in Europe, or VE Day. Ian Cameron, whose cycle and radio shop stood at the Cross, played records from his upstairs window, and all Neston, it seemed, danced under floodlights. Flags and bunting appeared on many buildings, and brass bands toured the district. There were many parties, both public and private. The Whiteways booked the town hall to celebrate with family and friends.

At the end of the war [Molly Roberts said] *there was a big party, tables in the field, and everyone gave what they could. We had a tin of pears on the*

The Neston branch of the British Legion marked Victory in Europe with an Olde Tyme Dance in the town hall.

Neston Sea Scouts paraded to celebrate the end of the war.

'invasion shelf'; anything extra went on this shelf in case we were invaded. The shelf was high up so we could not easily reach it.

The British Legion held an 'Olde Tyme Dance' at the town hall on 8 May, with the proceeds going towards their building fund. Japan surrendered on 14 August and the British Legion held another dance on VJ Day, celebrated on 15 and 16 August. Some Neston pubs ran out of beer, and cigarettes became scarce. There was again dancing at the floodlit Cross from dusk to midnight. The chairman of Neston Council, Frank Lewis, spoke to the crowd, who sang, *"There'll always be an England"*. The Ness Welcome Home Fund organized a carnival with sports and dancing. A series of children's parties was organized in the town hall, which was made available free of charge, and Willaston children were treated to fireworks and a bonfire by the British Legion. A further week of celebration was organized in October to coincide with National Savings Thanksgiving Week. Among other delights was an illuminated and decorated bus hired from Birkenhead.

Air raid wardens could look back on their five long years of responsibility as they passed Neston Cross.

Chapter Ten

Norman Thelwell sketched celebratory flags outside Dee Cottages and Sawyers Cottage in Parkgate.

For those who had grown up during the war, peace brought some surprises:

> *One of my lifelong memories* [said Bill Jones] *was when the blackout was lifted and to see all the gaily coloured curtains lit up and standing out like beacons, something that we just take for granted today.*

Gradually the soldiers were released from the forces and the long ordeal for their wives and families was over. One returning soldier was Bill Williams, who had joined the Territorial Army because, as a farm worker, he received no holidays, and the TA provided two weeks' camp a year which his employer had to allow. He fought at the ferocious battle for the German-held stronghold at Monte Cassino, where he was given a field commission and decorated, but he said that the ones who should have been awarded medals were the women back home, such as his wife Jenny, who had to bring up children on their own and endure years of worry. But for a few the strain had been too much, and not every homecoming was a happy one:

My marriage was finished [wrote another returning Neston soldier] *and I found myself a single person once again. Not my doing — far from it. I suppose not seeing the person I married in 1938, only four days in five years, didn't do the marriage any good.*

Thoughts soon turned towards ways of commemorating those who had served, but the desire of the British Legion for a new meeting place to replace the one they had used since the 1920s on Comrades Field, next to the parish church, had to wait until building materials were derestricted, and of course for funds to grow. They were able to buy the former Congregational chapel, next to the Institute, in 1946, and met there for twenty years before they could build their new clubhouse around it. In Willaston, where the War Memorial Hut had commemorated the First World War, the Institute was extended and renamed the Memorial Hall.

Those who had fallen in the First World War were remembered by providing the War Memorial Cottage Hospital in Little Neston. For those who died in the 1939–45 war, a 'Token of Remembrance' was planned at the library. In July 1947 Neston Council resolved that *"their very sincere thanks be extended to Mr Galloway for his most generous offer in presenting the land to the Council"*. It was decided that a sun lounge would be built at the rear of the library, with a garden of remembrance beside it. In early 1950 an appeal was launched, including a week of activities in April, followed by the news that a total of £785 had been raised, including £350 from the sale (to the St John's Ambulance Brigade branch at Winsford) of the ambulance which Mrs Higgin had provided at the start of the war. The sun lounge and the garden of remembrance were finally opened on 7 December 1953 by Mrs Olive Halewood, a councillor and past chairman of the council. Shortly afterwards, on 11 January 1954, a memorial screen bearing the names of those who had died was unveiled in Neston parish church by Mrs Charles Forsyth, whose son, Captain R. C. N. Forsyth, was named on the screen, to represent the parents of the fallen. A memorial (paid for from Mrs Higgin's ambulance) was also placed in the parish church of Burton, and the nine names for Willaston were inscribed on that village's existing war memorial.

The sun lounge lasted for only twenty years: it was demolished when the library was extended in 1973.

The conditions imposed by war took a long time to disperse. With the end of American aid in 1945, rationing actually became more severe, and bread was rationed for the first time. Rationing finally ended in 1953–4, the last item to be freed being meat in July 1954. Conscription continued

Chapter Ten

8th June, 1946

TO-DAY, AS WE CELEBRATE VICTORY, I send this personal message to you and all other boys and girls at school. For you have shared in the hardships and dangers of a total war and you have shared no less in the triumph of the Allied Nations.

I know you will always feel proud to belong to a country which was capable of such supreme effort; proud, too, of parents and elder brothers and sisters who by their courage, endurance and enterprise brought victory. May these qualities be yours as you grow up and join in the common effort to establish among the nations of the world unity and peace.

George R.I.

Another certificate — this time addressed to all the children who had experienced the grim years of war.

for longer as Britain's overseas commitments were slowly wound down. Men of 18, though not women, were called up for two years of National Service until 1960–2. Air raid shelters remained for even longer, for every attempt by Neston Council to demolish the eight public brick shelters was thwarted for many years. They attracted undesirable use, and although a few were used for such purposes as football changing rooms, most were a nuisance. But the Civil Defence authorities, with an eye on the Cold War, were unwilling to let them go. The need for housing development eventually overcame the policy for retention. The first was demolished in 1959 and the rest followed by about 1965.

One of the most pressing needs throughout the country was for houses, and it has been seen how the Nissen huts at Raby and Puddington were quickly occupied by squatters. The same thing happened at the hostels in Liverpool Road when they were vacated by the Navy. As soon as Neston Council heard that the Navy might be leaving, they enquired about the future of Neston camp, but were told that the War Office wanted it. Meanwhile, a group of local wives with husbands about to return from the forces took matters into their own hands. As one of them later related:

With Neston having no council houses to house them, it came to the ears of the young girls and their parents that HMS Mersey*, which is now the Ringway housing estate, was due to leave and Polish servicemen were coming in. One night in August 1945 they decided to cut the wire and squat in the huts. They were actually ordered out, but knowing how scarce houses were and would be, they decided to stay where they were. In doing so they called on old Mr Chrimes, Selwyn Lloyd* [the MP]*, Miss Bulley and the local midwife. They held a meeting and Selwyn Lloyd told them to get out, but the others told them to stay put.*

Neston Council had no wish to remove the squatters, and was concerned only to see that water and sanitation were adequate, and the War Office withdrew its claim when it learned that squatters were in occupation. By the end of that summer there were 51 names on the list of tenants. Neston Council was able to buy the land in October 1947, but began before then to refurbish the 50 buildings considered habitable. The huts were made into three-bedroom dwellings, with living room, bathroom and kitchen.

The rooms were bare brick and we put brown paper on the walls to cover them. They were very cold. Most of the couples stayed in the huts for eleven years before being rehoused in proper council houses. Despite all the trouble and aggravation, everybody was quite happy and content. The rent was 12s. 6d. a week.

Chapter Ten

Neston was allotted 25 aluminium prefabricated houses, called 'prefabs', originally intended for Little Neston, but while negotiating for the purchase of the Clayhill estate, the council sought and received permission to put the prefabs on that land next to the hostels. The land at the east end of the estate, where the naval camp had been, was being advertised as suitable for industry in 1953 — the start of the creation of the industrial estate, which still uses some of the naval barrack buildings. The hostels, though, were condemned as unsuitable for human habitation by the Medical Officer of Health in 1956 because they were seriously damp. He considered that the prefabs were not desirable but would do. Shortly after this the hostels began to be cleared.

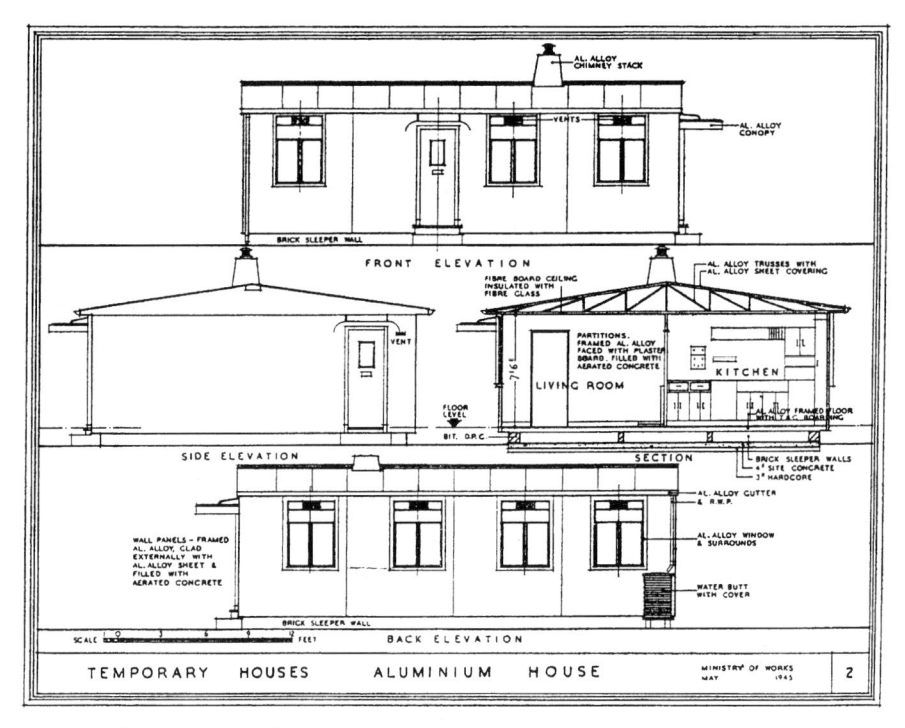

Neston Council, in common with many other towns and cities, erected temporary prefabricated houses to help ease the pressure for new homes.

Meanwhile, the council pressed ahead with house building, both private and public, as soon as materials became available. The need was not merely to house Nestonians, but also to allow for the growth in population that had been planned. The first post-war houses were built in two main groups: in Little Neston to the east of Burton Road, followed by a group in Neston south of Liverpool Road. In the first group, the building of Rose Gardens was shared among six different firms of local builders, in order to spread the work. Mellock Lane and Raeburn Avenue were built the same year; Morland and Landseer Avenues followed in 1950, Romney Way in 1951, Bendee Road in 1953–4 and Waterford Drive in 1955. The second group included Drake, Hawkins, Raleigh and Sidney Roads built in 1953–5, with Frobisher and Marlowe Roads in 1956, and Jonson, Spenser and Shakespeare Roads in 1957–8. Together with Breezehill Road, this latter group was completed in 1961. The Raby Road estate was built in 1953–4, and The Ringway was to follow in 1963–5 on the site of the hostels. The council had provided some five hundred houses by 1956.

The years after the First World War had been a considerable disappointment to the returning soldiers, because Lloyd George's promise *"to make Britain a fit country for heroes to live in"* was not fulfilled. There was therefore a determination, even in the early years of the Second World War, that constructive use must be made, when peace finally came, of the spirit of national unity which the war engendered.

The ready acceptance of close Government control and radical change which war conditions made necessary also encouraged some to think that similar conditions could be applied in peacetime. Although Churchill himself devoted all his energies to winning the war and spared little time or interest to the problems of peace, many of the ministers in his coalition Government pursued visions of a better future. There was therefore a general welcome in December 1942 to the publication of the Beveridge Report, which laid down the principles of the welfare state. Sir William Beveridge, civil servant, academic and later a Liberal MP, chaired a committee charged with reforming social insurance — for pensions, unemployment and health. His report proposed that all three, with family allowances and other benefits, should be combined in one compulsory contribution. The report assumed a National Health Service would be established, following an Emergency Health Scheme which operated during the war. A unified health service had been proposed by another committee in 1942. Similarly in education, the Norwood Committee proposed in 1943 that secondary education should be provided for all, and this was embodied in the Education Act of 1944. Another wartime initiative, the Town & Country Planning Act of 1943, was also to affect radically the shape of the coming peace. All these plans were summed up in Beveridge's vision of the end of Want, Disease, Squalor, Ignorance and Idleness.

Admirable though this vision was, not every change imposed on Neston was for the better: some hopes took a long time to fulfil, and some could not be achieved at all. One of the first effects of these reforms in Neston concerned the cottage hospital, established in 1920 as a war memorial, and supported ever since, sometimes with great difficulty, by subscriptions, raffles, whist drives and donations. In 1948 it was absorbed by the new National Health Service and ceased to be truly local. As the hospital's report for 1947–8 said,

> While all will wish the new Health Service success in its vast undertaking, there remains for many of us a real regret at the passing of a service which has become dear and familiar, and which has played so important a part in our lives.

The report acknowledged that the financial burden was becoming intolerable, and *"This burden of maintenance, hitherto borne by a section of the public, will in future be laid on the back of the British people as a whole."* But the financial viability of a small hospital with only 25 beds was always in doubt, and the NHS closed it in 1964.

The return of normal family life was bound to increase the child population, and the need to improve the local school system became urgent. Neston had long felt the need for a secondary school, and a field beside Mellock Lane had been bought for that purpose in 1931. But that site was too small and was eventually used for St Winefride's primary school and the health clinic. The 1944 Education Act promised secondary education of three kinds: grammar, modern and technical. The old elementary schools, which had taken children up to the school-leaving age of 14, were to be shorn of their pupils over 11 and become primary schools. There were six elementary schools in the Neston UDC area, and most of them were crowded, a problem made worse by the raising of the school-leaving age to 15 in 1948 and the large number of new houses being built. The 1944 Act allowed for a further rise in the leaving age to 16, although this did not happen until 1973. The intention seems to have been to concentrate the pupils over 11 at the Burton Road school, which was by far the largest, but this did not happen because the school ran out of space, despite using the former Baptist chapel in Bushell Road, and Salem Hall in Burton Road, as overflow classrooms.

Huge numbers of new schools had to be built, and Neston kept on finding itself at the back of the queue: Cheshire built 51 schools before

Neston's. Neston Council hoped to use an existing building, and nominated the former Leighton Girls' School, on sale in April 1946 after being vacated by the Army. Another suggestion was to use Leighton Court, both houses having plenty of land at the time. But the county council rejected these and bought a site in Raby Park Road, near the High Road. For years Neston Council pestered both Chester and Whitehall to start work on the new school. In 1950 they pleaded that their new industrial recruit, Morgan Crucible, needed technically skilled labour. In 1953 they complained that neighbouring districts had been given schools already but would not allow Neston children to go to them. Actually some Neston children did go to the new secondary schools at Pensby and Sutton, and Roman Catholic children could go to Bebington.

At last Neston's new school opened in January 1958, with the official opening six months later. It was a secondary modern and technical school. But those Neston children who sought a grammar school education still had to travel elsewhere, mainly to Calday Grange or West Kirby High School. This problem was not solved until 1972, when Neston County Secondary School became comprehensive, and the three types of school envisaged in 1944 were merged into one.

Of all the wartime visions for the future, it was the Town & Country Planning Act which made the most difference. In 1945 the population of Neston Urban District, which included Burton and Willaston, was nearly 9,000. A Merseyside commission appointed under the Act proposed that Neston's population should rise to 20,000. Josephine Reynolds, planning assistant to the Neston UDC, wrote an 'outline plan' for Neston in which she suggested that, to achieve this growth without disturbing the nature of the place, the increase should take place over 150 years. Of course, the luxury of so much time was not available, and Neston inevitably changed under the pressure of the newcomers.

Even before the influx of new faces began, Neston had problems in providing sufficient work. In 1945, when there were hundreds away in the forces, about half the working population were employed outside the district. The returning servicemen had to be offered their old jobs back, where they had any, but the need for more job opportunities in Neston itself was urgent. Neston Council therefore allocated for industry 110 acres of land to the north of Liverpool Road, stretching from the brickworks by Leighton Road to Clayhill, where the naval camp still stood. Miss Reynolds thought this far too large an area, and suggested only 25 acres for the moment, with 20 in reserve. In the end the only large

Chapter Ten

employer who moved into this industrial area was the Morgan Crucible company, makers of graphite crucibles for use in foundries, and clay assay goods for use in laboratories and industry. This firm, from London, showed interest in moving to Neston from 1946, and actually established itself three years later.

After the war, the Morgan Crucible company was the only large employer to move into the area which Neston had allocated for industry, to the north of Liverpool Road.

If Miss Reynolds had had her way, Neston would have been changed much more radically by her outline plan. She would have removed most of the traffic from the High Street, bypassing Neston on three sides. She proposed to continue Liverpool Road through what were then fields to Buggen Lane; to extend Hinderton Road along the line of the railway to Parkgate; and to make a main road on the east side of the town along the line of Bushell and Breezehill Roads. At Parkgate, the Parade would be freed of traffic by driving roads on both sides of the railway line. Willaston would have a bypass on its north side.

She had even greater plans for the centre of Neston. She considered the town hall to be *"hard to find"*, and proposed a new square at the head of the High Street, with an imposing new town hall where the Methodist church stands. The site of Leighton Court would become a youth and leisure centre, with swimming pool, gymnasium, cinema and so on. All these ambitious changes were far too expensive for the council to take seriously, and most of the plan remains an expression of hope. But the vision which Miss Reynolds expressed was typical of the feeling, in Neston as elsewhere, that the successful end of the war was offering all of us a new and promising start.

Chapter Ten

SOURCES

This chapter was written by Geoffrey Place.

Susan Chambers researched the hostels at Clayhill, the victory celebrations, the library memorial and post-war house building.

Josephine Reynolds, *An Outline Plan for Neston Urban District* (1946); Neston & District War Memorial Cottage Hospital, *Annual Report 1947–48*; and Greg Dawson, *Wyrale — Wirral Topics* were among the publications consulted.

We are grateful for the memories of Roy Booth, Bill Jones, Henry Peters, Molly Roberts, Norman Thelwell, Arnold Whiteway and Bill Williams (via Greg Dawson).

INDEX

Note: Service units will be found under the main headings of Army, Royal Air Force, and Royal Navy. Aerodromes, hospitals, and schools and staff are also grouped together rather than shown under their respective locations. An underlined figure indicates that the reference is to a caption, but if it also applies to the narrative on the same page then only one figure is shown, not underlined.

aerodromes
    Cranage, Holmes Chapel, 32, 33
    Hawarden, 31, 38, 131
    High Ercall, Salop, 38
    Hooton Park, 29, 38, 131
    Little Sutton, 29, 131
    Moreton-in-Marsh, 38
    Poulton, 131
    Sealand, 29, 31, 36, 37, 38, 39, 131, 132
    Speke, 31, 37
    Squires Gate, Blackpool, 32, 35
AFS. *See* Auxiliary Fire Service
Air Raid Precautions (ARP), 3, 4, 5, 6, 33, 43, 44, 46, 48, 50, 51, 52, 57, 60
    fire guards, 48, 57, 63
    fire-watchers, 50, 61, 63, 116
    messengers, 116
    wardens, 2, 3, 42, 48, 50, 52, 57, 58, 60, 63, 65, 83, 153
air raid(s), 1, 6, 7, 9, 11, 15, 23, 27, 32, 35, 42, 43, 45, 48, 52, 53, 54, 55, 60, 63, 68, 75, 76, 80, 81, 85, 131, 144
    shelter marshals, 50
    shelters, 6, 7, 21, 23, 24, 42, 43, 44, 45, 46, 47, 48, 49, 50, 52, 54, 57, 68, 116, 157
    sirens, 41, 46, 50, 52, 63
aircraft
    British
        Airspeed Oxford, 39
        Avro
            Anson, 29, 38
            Lancaster, 36, 111, 114
        Blackburn Botha, 38

        Boulton Paul Defiant, 32, 35
        Bristol
            Beaufighter, 30, 36
            Blenheim, 146
        de Havilland
            Mosquito, 30, 38
            Tiger Moth, 29, 30, 36, 37
        Fairey Swordfish, 39
        Hawker
            Hind, 29
            Hurricane, 30, 31, 32, 33, 36, 37
        Miles Master, 29
        Vickers
            Supermarine Spitfire, 29, 30, 31, 32, 38, 68
            Wellington, 29, 36, 38, 111, 144
    German
        Dornier Do17, 31
        Heinkel He111, 31, 33, 35, 36
        Junkers Ju88, 31, 35, 36, 68, 121
allotments, 95
Anderson shelter. *See* air raid shelters
Anderson, Sir John, 57
Anfield, 47
anti-aircraft batteries, 35, 42, 53, 55, 75, 76, 77, 78, 79, 80, 100
Army
    38th (Welsh) Division, 127
    Cheshire (Earl of Chester's) Yeomanry, 128
    Cheshire Regiment, 84, 128, 130
    Green Howards, 128
    King's Own Royal Regiment, 144
    Lancashire Fusiliers, 144, 145

Index

Army (*continued*)
    Royal Army Service Corps, 140
    Royal Artillery, 75, 77, 78, 79, 96, 130.
        See also anti-aircraft batteries
    Royal Corps of Signals, 146
    Royal Engineers, 120, 130
    Royal Horse Artillery, <u>68</u>, 147
    Royal Northumberland Fusiliers, 36, 55, 127, 128
    Royal Observer Corps, 33, 78
    Royal Tank Regiment, 146
    Western Command, 130, 131
ARP. *See* Air Raid Precautions
Arrowe Park, 78, 131
Ascanius, 141
Ashfield
    Farm, 96
    Hall Farm, 24, 96, 128, <u>129</u>, 130, 135
ATS. *See* Auxiliary Territorial Service
Auxiliary Fire Service (AFS), 57, 60, 61, 62
Auxiliary Territorial Service (ATS), 77, 79, 110, 139

Barlow, Marcus H., & Co., 23
barrage balloons, 75, 80
Bates, Sir Percy, 61
Bebington, 31, 100
    Food Office, 98
Bennett, Rev. Frank, 21
Betws-y-Coed, 24
Bidston, 65, 76
Birkenhead, 7, 14, 23, 35, 41, 52, 62, 65, 67, 80, 100, 118, 119, 128, 153
    Fire Service, 61
Birkenhead Advertiser, 31
Birkenhead News, 4, 60, 65
Birmingham, 80
black market, 103
blackout, 14, 32, 45, 48, 57, 58, 67, 96, 109, 110, 116, 154
Blacon cemetery, 38
Bolton, 20, 22
bombing practice, 29
bombs
    flying, 27, 131

    high-explosive, <u>5</u>, 32, 41, 52, 53
    incendiary, <u>5</u>, 15, 33, 41, 47, 52, 53, 54, 55, 60, 61, 62, 68, 81, 116, 124, 128, 130
Bootle, 6
Boston, G. S., 65, 87
Brimstage, 74
British Legion, <u>152</u>, 153, 155
British Restaurants, 104, 107
Bromborough, 78, 133
    Dock, 31
Broughton, 111, <u>112</u>, 113
Bulley, Lois, 20, 157
Burton, 12, 48, 54, 68, 71, 76, 80, 83, 85, 87, 92, 104, 124, 135, 148, 161
    Dunstan Lane, 54
    Gladstone Village Hall, 12
    Manor, 41, 71, 130, 133
    marshes, 29, 38, 53, 54, 81, 96
    parish church of St Nicholas, 155
    Stanley House, 44
    Stone House, 44
    Vicarage Lane, 37

Caldy, 74
Canada, 25, 26, 104
Capenhurst, 86, 112, 113
Cerrigydrudion, 27, 102
Cheshire County Council, 6, 65, 80, 161
Chester, 21, 29, 35, 68, 100, 101, 113, 114, 124, 127, 130
    Border House Farm, 31
    Castle, 131
Chester High Road, 24, 87, 96, 98, 113, 128
Childer Thornton, 74
City of Benares, 27
Civil Defence, 6, 11, 42, 48, 57, 110, 157
Clatterbridge, 110, 134
Colwyn Bay, 124
conscientious objectors, 33, 100, 139
Coventry, 7

Daily Mail, 140
decoy targets, 53, 54, 55, 75, 81
Denhall, 74

Index

Old Quay House, 75
Denhall Lane, 81

Eccles, 16, 20
Edwards, Rev. J. Russell, 55, 63, 135, <u>136</u>, 139, 141, 146
employment, 161
evacuation, <u>2</u>, 6, 8, 11, 12, 14, 15, 16, <u>18</u>, 20, 21, 22, 23, 24, 27, 41, 64, 65, 67, 68, 69, 71, 76
Exton, Horby, 139

farming, 95, 96, <u>99</u>, 100, 115
Fisher, Sir Warren, 50, 52, 57
Five Ways garage, 113
Flint, 36
   Bank, 38
foot and mouth disease, 96
fund-raising schemes, 31, 33, 34, 68, 121, 131, 153, 155

gas, 1, 2, 3, <u>5</u>, 46, 50, 64, 68
   masks, 2, 3, 45, 48, 60
Greasby, 121
Grenfell, Mrs Erma, 102
Grenfell, Sir Wilfred, 24
Guernsey, 11, 16, 17, <u>18</u>, 20, 21, 22, 23, 76
   Les Cotils convent school, 17
   St Saviour's School, 16, 17
Gunn, 2nd Lt George Ward, VC, MC, 67, <u>68</u>, 138, 146, 147, 148
Gunn, Dr George, 67, 147

Hawarden, 11, 29, 111
Heswall, 11, 24, 33, 41, 46, 55, 61, 81, 82, 101
Higgin, Major W. W., 87, 134
Higgin, Mrs Olive, 65, 155
Hilbre Islands, 33, 81
Hinderton, 15
   cross-roads, 60
   Hall, 61
   Shrewsbury Arms, 103
   The Mount, 15, 87
Home Guard, 4, 15, 30, 31, 32, 33, 36, 37, 73, <u>74</u>, 75, 77, 81, 82, <u>83</u>, 84, 85, 86, 87, <u>88</u>, 89, 110, 116
Hooton, 76, 97, 112, 113, 134
   station, 113
Horsman, Victor, 23, 114
hospitals
   Barrowmore, Delamore Forest, 61
   Chester Royal Infirmary, 12
   Clatterbridge
      American military, 68, 133, 134
      fever, 67
      general, 37, 64, 67, 69
   David Lewis Northern, Liverpool, 131
   Eaton Hall, military, 131
   Leasowe children's, 104
   Moston, military, 131
   Neston cottage, 20, 64, 67, 105, 148, 155, 160
   Thornton Manor, 68
housing, 71, 113, 114, 157, 158, 159, 160
Hoylake, 24, 61, 75

identity cards, 87, 94, 124
Ince, 76
Irby, 21

Lancashire, 16
Land Girls. *See* Women's Land Army
Leahurst veterinary field station, 24, 98
Ledsham, 74, 75, 76, 87, 100, 134, 135
Leeman's Printers, 23
Lever estate, 24, 130
Leverhulme, 2nd Viscount, 25
lighting regulations, 50, 57, 58, 60
Little Neston, 8, 22, 32, 36, 39, 53, 67, 76, 83, <u>84</u>, 86, 89, 92, 119, 135, 155, 158, 159
   Badger Bait, 44, 54, 119
   Bendee Road, 159
   Bull Hill, 53
   Burton Road, 17, 95, 119, 133, 159, 160
   Harp Inn, 38, 54
   Ivy Farm, 46
   Landseer Avenue, 159

Index

Little Neston (*continued*)
    Lees Lane, 30, 87
    Marshlands Road, 38, 95, 102
    Mellock Lane, 23, 53, 54, 159, 160
    Methodist chapel, <u>140</u>
    Morland Avenue, 159
    New Street, 44
    Newtown, 53
    post office, 4
    Raeburn Avenue, 159
    Romney Way, 159
    Rose Gardens, 119, 159
    Royal Oak, 63
    St Winefride's church, 8, 12
        hall, 12, 17
    Town Lane, 44
    Victoria Road, 54, 76
    Waterford Drive, 159
    West Vale, 23, 38, 39
    Woodfall Lane, 38, 54, 76
Little Sutton, 82, 87, 104, 113
Liverpool, 2, 6, 7, 11, 15, 21, 23, 24, 27, 30, 32, 33, 35, 46, 52, 53, 55, 62, 75, 76, 77, 100, 101, 106, 113, 114, 118, 119, 124, 127, 128, 130, 131, 139, 140
    Bay, 8, 100, 101
    docks, 35, 61, 131
    University, 24, 98
    Walker Art Gallery, 24
Liverpool Daily Post, 58, 110
Liverpool Echo, 47, 118
Local Defence Volunteers. *See* Home Guard
London, 7, 11, 14, 27, 32, 52, 57, 62, 124, 131, 144, 162
Lytham St Annes, 124

Manchester, 16, 124, 130
Maresco family, 65
maternity hostels, 65
Maurita, 101
Merseyside, 7, 11, 15, 27, 32, 33, 52, 55, 64, 67, 75, 76, 131, 161
military decorations, 67, 138, 146, 147, 154
Mollington, 114

Morgan Crucible, 161, 162
Morrison shelter. *See* air raid shelters
Morrison, Herbert, 57

NAAFI. *See* Navy, Army & Air Force Institutes
Nantwich, 15, 95
National Economy Salvage Fuels, 23
National Fire Service (NFS), 62
National Savings, 121, <u>122</u>, 153
National Service, 68, 157
Navy, Army & Air Force Institutes, 77, 130
Ness, 8, 44, 85, 116, 119, 135, 153
    Goldstraw Farm, 54, 81
    Mill Lane, 44
    Oddfellows Hall, 23, 133
    Snab Lane, 38
Ness Gardens, 98
Neston
    and district Council of Social Service, 95
    and Parkgate Laundry, 4, 23, 27
    Blackeys Lane, 45, 53
    Breezehill Road, 159, 162
    Bridge Street, 44, 68, 118
    Buggen Lane, 53, 73, 162
    Bushell Road, 160, 162
    Chester Road, 68
    Church Lads' Club, 63, 135, <u>136</u>
    Church Lane, 73
    Clayhill, 27, 131, 158, 161
    Comrades Field, <u>136</u>, 155
    Congregational hall (formerly chapel), 12, 155
    cottage hospital. *See* hospitals
    Cross, 44, 48, 52, 60, 65, 73, 110, 151, 153
    Cross Street, 23, 61
    Drake Road, 159
    Elm Grove House, 53
    fire brigade, 60, 71
    fire station, 60, 61, 62
    Food Control Committee, 91, 94, 107
    Food Office, 91, 92, 93, 94, 95, 103, 104, 106

Index

Frobisher Road, 159
Gladstone Road, 120
Hawkins Road, 159
High Street, 44, 162
Hinderton Road, 23, 31, 54, 63, 162
    The Garth, 65
Hotel, 15, 50
Institute, 14, 15, 17, 20, 64, 76, 128, 133, 155
Jackson's tower, 44
Jonson Road, 159
Kelly's Buildings, 68
Leighton Court, 15, 53, 64, 161, 163
Leighton Road, 15, 17, 23, 109, 114, 161
library, 53, 155
Liverpool Road, 131, 157, 159, 161, 162
Marlowe Road, 159
Mayfield Gardens, 44, <u>45</u>, 139
Methodist church, 53, 162
Moorside Lane, 15, 139
New Cinema, 21, 61, 95
old police station, 64
Old Quay Lane, 23, 27
Olive Drive, 53
parish church of St Mary and St Helen, 21, 63, 119, 148, 155
    hall, 64
Park Street, 64
Parkgate Road, 48, 53, 73, 121
police station, 33, 41, 63, 64, 81, 118
Presbyterian church, 53, 128
Public Health Officer. *See* Prince, Andrew
Raby Park Road, 161
Raby Road estate, 159
Raleigh Road, 159
Ringway estate, 157, 159
Sewing for the Forces class, 69
Shakespeare Road, 159
Sidney Road, 159
Spenser Road, 159
Stanney Park, 121
Talbot Avenue, 44
Tanks Field, 120

The Vaults, 12
Town Clerk. *See* Poole, Frank
town hall, 12, 15, 16, 20, 21, 41, <u>47</u>, 50, 60, 63, 64, 65, 68, 71, 91, 118, 128, 153, 162
Urban District Council, <u>2</u>, 3, 6, 8, 12, 23, 42, 44, 46, 47, 48, 50, 63, 64, 65, 73, 78, 95, 101, 110, 116, 118, 119, 120, 130, 153, 155, 157, 158, 159, 161, 163
War Comforts committee, 70
New Brighton, 15
New Ferry, 15, 136
NFS. *See* National Fire Service

Order of St John of Jerusalem, <u>70</u>

Parkgate, 6, 8, 11, 12, 14, 15, 23, 24, 27, 31, 33, 36, 37, 41, 53, 67, 68, 73, 74, 75, 76, 81, 92, 101, 102, 114, 116, 121, 128, 130, 131, 132, 133, 135, 136, 162
    Balcony House, 44
    Bevyl Road, 31, 76, 95, 127
    Boat House Café, 36, 55, 128
    Boathouse Lane, 38, 76, 116, 128
    Brookland Road, 44
    Dee Cottages, <u>154</u>
    Deeside Café, 104
    Earle Drive, 91
    fishermen, 94, 100, 101, 103
    Hotel, 32, 127
    Manorial Road, 24
        Ashburton, 65, 127
    Mostyn Gardens, 62, 95
    Parade, 31, 33, 62, 63, 114, 162
    Parks Field, 73, 96, 132
    post office, 4, 63
    Sawyers Cottage, <u>154</u>
    Sea View, 44
    station, 92, 101
    Station Road, <u>74</u>
    swimming baths, 20, 43, 55, 62, 128
    The Runnel, 39, 100
    Union Hotel, 104
    Wood Lane, 52, 76, 91, 131, 132, 139
        Woodcote, 55, 128

Index

pillboxes, 4, 73, 74, 75, 76
Plymouth, 7
Poole, Frank, 11, 52, 57, 62, 65, 91, 92, 95, 121, 127
Port Sunlight, 31, 74
Poulton, 11
prefabs. *See* housing
Prenton, 4, 52
Prince, Andrew, 33, 38, 39, 53, 65, 101, 121
prisoners of war, 31, 32, 33, 36, 100, 106, 128, 133, 134, 135, 138, 140
Puddington, 41, 42, 76, 77, 78, 79, 80, 87, 96, 104, 124, 139, 144, 157
    Hall, 65, 71, 134
    Home Farm, 96, 98

Raby, 21, 41, 42, 52, 73, 76, 77, 78, 97, 134, 139, 157
    Blakeley Road, 41
    Corner House Farm, 15
    Willow Brow Farm, 46, 55, 77, 80, 96
radar, 37, 75, 76, 77, 80, 136
RAF. *See* Royal Air Force
rationing, 91, 92, 93, 94, 98, 100, 101, 102, 103, 104, 107, 109, 114, 155
Reaseheath Agricultural College, 95, 98, 104, 124
Red Cross, 2, 20, 21, 47, 63, 64, 65, 69, 70, 71, 106
refugees, 24, 104
road blocks, 4, 73, 87
Rock Ferry, 23
Roften. *See* Royal Ordnance factories
Royal Air Force, 4, 29, 31, 32, 36, 38, 80, 85, 131, 144, 146
    No.96 Squadron, 33
    No.99 Squadron, 144
    No.256 Squadron, 35
    No.307 Squadron, 35
    No.312 Squadron, 31
    No.610 (County of Chester) Squadron, 29
Royal Navy, 39, 131, 141, 142, 145, 157
    HM Gunboat 87, 124
    HMS *Aphis*, 141, 142

HMS *Conway*, 23, 41
HMS *Galatea*, 141
HMS *Juno*, 142
HMS *Kimberley*, 148
HMS *Mersey*, 131, 157
HMS *Taku*, 8
HMS *Thetis*, 7
Royal New Zealand Air Force, 38
Royal Ordnance factories, 86, 112, 113, 134
Rural District Pie Scheme, 107, 124
Rushworth & Dreaper, 24

Saighton, 131
Salford, 130
salvage, 48, 118, 120, 121
sandbags, 47, 76
Saughall, 128
schools and staff
    Bebington, 161
    Bishop Wilson's, Burton, 12
    Booker, H. S., 12, 20
    Burton Road, 6, 17, 20, 42, 64, 110, 115, 120, 121, 139, 160
    Byrne, Kathleen, 14
    Calday Grange, 86, 161
    Congregational chapel, 20
    Davies, J. R., 114
    Elleray Park, Wallasey, 12, 15
    Exton, A. J., 101, 115, 121
    Fowles, G. H., 121
    Greasby infants', 22
    Grenfell, A. M. D., 6, 24, 25, 26, 42, 43, 44, 46, 58, 62, 65, 98, 103, 110, 127
    Hacking, J., 64
    Helm, W. J., 106
    Leighton Girls', Parkgate, 8, 55, 127, 128, 161
    Les Cotils, Guernsey, 17
    Lever, Thornton Hough, 130
    Liverpool Road, 2, 22, 27, 42, 104, 121
    Millington, Miss, 12
    Moorland House, Heswall, 24

Index

Mostyn House, 6, <u>7</u>, 11, 23, 24, 27, 41, 42, 43, 44, 55, 58, 62, 67, 93, 95, 102, 103, 110, 121, 124, 128, 147
Ness Holt, 29, 42, 52, 114, 115
Neston
    County Secondary, 161
    Institute, 17, 20
Ogle, Nurse, 12
Orde, Mr, 12
Parkgate infants', 42, 50
Pensby secondary, 161
Piper, Miss, 14
Poulton, 11
Raby Park Road, 22
Rigby House, Parkgate, 12, 15, 133
Riverside, 11
St Saviour's, Guernsey, 16, 17
St Winefride's, 17, 54, 160
Sutton secondary, 161
Taylor, Miss R., 12, 15
The Leas, Hoylake, 24
Thornton Hough, 22, 118
Torode, Ada, 17, 20, 22
Vining, Gerald, 15, 16, 17, 20
Wallasey, 11
West Kirby High, 161
Willaston, 12, 62, 106
Wirral Grammar, 134
Woodfall Lane, 30
Seacombe, 11
Sealand, 86, 87
searchlight batteries, 71, 75, 76, 105, 116, 127
'seavacuees', 24, 27
Shakespeare, Geoffrey, MP, 26
Shotton steelworks, 30, 46, 81, 96
Shute, Sir John, MP, 25, 26
squatters, 78, 80, 157
St Helens, 20
Storeton, 130

Tacoma City, 23
Thornton Hough, 24, 130
    Congregational church, 133
    Westwood Grange, 130
Thornton Manor, 41, 130

Thurstaston, 33, 75, 76, 101
town planning, 161, 162, 163
Tranmere Laundry, 23
Twickenham, 71

United Molasses, 23
Upton by Chester, 76

Victory, 65
victory celebrations, 151
Viking, 16
Vining, Mrs, 20

WAAF. *See* Women's Auxiliary Air Force
Wallasey, 7, 11, 12, 14, 15, 16, 20, 24, 53, 61, 67
Walsh, J. J., Ltd, 23
War Agricultural Executive Committee (War Ag), 95, 96, <u>97</u>, 98, 100, 104, 124
war memorials, 155, 160
Warrington, 120
Warwick Castle, 128
West Harrow, 27
West Kirby, 31, 131
Widnes, 33
wildfowling, 30, 102
Willaston, 8, 14, 15, 27, 41, 65, 68, 69, 71, 75, 76, 87, 92, 98, 102, 104, 106, 113, 114, 116, 135, 148, 153, 161, 162
    church hall, 12
    Hadlow Wood, 87
    Hanns Hall Farm, 98
    Institute, 107, 155
    Memorial Hall, 107, 155
    Midland Bank, 44
    Raby Farm, 37
    Raby House Farm, 41
    war memorial, 155
    War Memorial Hut, 41, 68, 107, 155
    Woodcroft Farm, 37
    Young Farmers' Club, 118
Wirral Refugee Committee, 24
Women's Auxiliary Air Force (WAAF), 110

Women's Institutes, 57, 68, 71, 104, 105, 106, 107, 124
Women's Land Army, 71, 100
Women's Royal Naval Service (WRNS), 110, 139, 142, 144
Women's Voluntary Service (WVS), 17, 20, 21, 31, 57, <u>58</u>, 68, 71, 92, 104, 106, 107, 120
Woolwich, 113
Wrexham, 14
WRNS. *See* Women's Royal Naval Service
WVS. *See* Women's Voluntary Service
Wychbold, Worcs., 35

Yeoman, Dr J. B., 12, 27, 48, 53, 121
youth organizations, <u>99</u>, 106, 116, 118, 141, <u>152</u>